PROJECT SELF-ESTEEM
For Kids

WENDY CULLUM

WESTBOW
PRESS
A DIVISION OF THOMAS NELSON
& ZONDERVAN

WestBow Press books may be ordered through booksellers or by contacting:

WestBow Press
A Division of Thomas Nelson & Zondervan
1663 Liberty Drive
Bloomington, IN 47403
www.westbowpress.com
1 (866) 928-1240

ISBN: 978-1-4908-1145-1 (sc)
ISBN: 978-1-4908-1146-8 (e)

Library of Congress Control Number: 2013918416

Printed in the United States of America.

WestBow Press rev. date: 04/15/2014

PREFACE

I've always loved children. When I was a teenager, I babysat every weekend. I looked forward to being married and being a mother someday. I have been fortunate to have found a wonderful man and have 4 beautiful children.

When my oldest son started school I wanted to volunteer any chance I could in his classrooms. There was a program at the school for a parent to teach subjects once a month that would help children raise their self-esteem. I enjoyed teaching it so much that I continued for 10 years. The program became dated and so I decided to use my own ideas to supplement.

When the school was considering dropping the program I stepped up and asked if I could rewrite it. My offer was accepted and it took me 3 yrs to perfect the lessons and here is my program "project-self esteem for kids".

ACKNOWLEDGEMENTS

I would like to say thank you to Eileen Kostyk for trusting me to take over and write my own lessons.

I would also like to thank some of the faithful mothers (my friends) who have helped teach the lessons at Butterfield; Marlo, Tangi, Nori, Misty, Christina, Vicky, Julie, Tish, and Susie.

Without my beautiful children this book would not go forth. I love you Jacob, Chandler, Travis, and Paige.

To my husband Larry, I love you more than anything, and you have always been my biggest supporter.

To my sister, Pamela, I thank you for always being my inspiration and paving the way for new adventures.

To my parents who love me and have always tried to meet my needs, wants, and wishes, I love you!

Thank you, Barbara, for your beautiful drawings and Julie for your amazing photography.

Psalms. 127:3

INTRODUCTION

This program is designed to help children raise their self-esteem. It is very versatile and can be taught in homes and schools.

For the use in schools a coordinator is essential. This person will find and be in contact with each parent volunteer who will be teaching the lessons. The coordinator will be in charge of keeping a supply closet with binders for each class with the lessons inside and the necessary materials needed. The parent volunteer will go to the supply closet each month before teaching to review the lesson and retrieve supplies that are needed.

The teachers appreciate the life lessons being taught each month and the students have a great time participating!

I will gladly use my expertise and experience to assist any school in developing this amazing program. Feel free to comment and request info at Wendy1970@verizon.net.

W I S D O M

Objectives
-Introduce Spotlight –
-Discuss the meaning of wisdom and introduce "Kids Catching Kids" box
-Discuss Situation Cards
-Chalkboard activity using Silhouette
-Discuss famous people using wisdom
-Discuss quote

Materials
-A journal for every student
-3-4 pieces of construction paper for Spotlights
-Box labeled "Kids Catching Kids"
-Situation cards- (8-3X5 cards with scenarios listed in lesson)
-Silhouette for each student

Activity A–Introduction of facilitator, Project Self-Esteem, and Spotlight

Tell the students your name and a little bit about yourself and that you are here to teach Project Self-Esteem. Self-esteem is how you feel about yourself. If you feel good about yourself, you will be happy and will treat others well. Explain that your goal is to teach them to have good self-esteem through these lessons. Tell them that each one of them is special and this year you are going to find out why.

Pass out a journal to each student and ask them to write their name on the front cover. Tell the students that these journals are for them to take notes in during each of your lessons. Explain that when they take notes they will better remember what you have taught, and they will have their notes to refer to at the last lesson where you will have a review of the entire year. Now have the students open to the first page and write the date. Number the lines 1 to 10. Ask the 10 following questions and have them write their answers.

1. What is your favorite color?
2. What is your favorite food?
3. What is your favorite restaurant?
4. What is your favorite movie or T.V. show?
5. What is your favorite sport?
6. What is your favorite thing to do in your free time?
7. What is a talent that you have?
8. Where is a place that you would like to visit?
9. What would you like to be when you grow up?
10. Who is a person you admire? (dead or alive)

When you are done asking these questions, tell the students that you are going to play a game called Spotlight with them at the end of the lesson. Have them turn to the next page and tell them they will be taking notes throughout the lesson.

Activity B–Discuss the meaning of wisdom and introduce the box labeled "Kids Catching Kids"

Tell the students that today you are going to discuss the meaning of wisdom. Write the word on the board. Ask them if they know the definition. After the discussion, write the definition on the board. **Wisdom is knowing what you need to do and choosing to do it**. Have the students copy this definition into their journal.

Read the following. We know lots of things don't we? We know we should be courteous to others, but sometimes we are not. We know we should be polite and use good manners, but sometimes we don't. We know we should eat things that are good for our bodies, but sometimes we don't. Wisdom is about more than just storing information. It's about more than just learning facts and gaining knowledge. Wisdom is the next step. It is about using what you learn.

Place the box labeled "Kids Catching Kids" where all students can see it. Tell the students that the box will be left in the classroom the entire month to catch students making smart choices. Tell the students that they will be watching for other students making good choices. Then they are to write on a piece of paper the student's name and the good choice they made and place it in the box. (Examples might be, seeing someone picking up trash or being a friend to someone who seems lonely.) Tell the students that at the next lesson, you will open the box and read the papers to see who has been using their wisdom.

Activity C–Discussion using "Situation Cards"

Using 8- 3x5 cards, write each one of the following situations below to be passed out to 8 selected students.

1. You accidently leave your lunch at home.
2. You find a large sum of money on the playground.
3. Your best friend ignores you at recess.
4. You get separated from your family at the mall.
5. You hear a strange sound in the middle of the night.
6. You break your friend's favorite toy.
7. Someone calls you a mean name.
8. Your teacher writes you a note telling you what a great job you did today.

Pass out cards and tell them that each situation is in need of a solution. Have each student read their card out loud and tell how they would use wisdom in reacting to each situation.

Activity D–Chalkboard activity using Silhouettes

Draw a line down the center of the chalkboard. On the left side, write the title "What I Know". Pass out a silhouette to each student. Have the students write their name at the bottom of the silhouette. Tell each student to write down something that they have learned in the center. (Some examples might be; dance, read, play sports, etc.) Collect all of the silhouettes and hang them under the title, "What I Know". Then on the right side of the chalkboard write the title, "What I Do With What I Know". Lead a discussion about how their talents will lead to short and long-term goals. (For example; if a student wrote "dance" on their silhouette, then you might write "perform in a recital" under the title "What I do With What I Know".

Activity E–Read about a famous person using wisdom

Mother Teresa (1910-1997)

Teresa was born in Macedonia. Her father was an Albanian grocer. In 1928, she became a Roman Catholic nun. In 1929, she went to India and taught high school in Calcutta. She left school to work with the poor in Calcutta and took an intensive nursing course. She started an open-air school in a park in a poor neighborhood. Two years later Teresa founded the Missionaries of Charity, requiring that anyone joining them must commit themselves to work with the poorest of the poor and not receive any money for their work. In the following years, Missionaries of Charity houses were opened around the world in such places as Tanzania, Rome, Venezuela, Australia, Israel, Peru, Mexico, and New York. Teresa received prestigious awards from the governments of India, Great Britain and the United Nations. In 1979, she received the Nobel Peace Prize for her work with the poor around the world. There are now over 1,500 Missionaries of Charity who have helped over 6,000,000 people around the world.

Lead a discussion on how Mother Teresa is a great example of how someone can use their wisdom to help others and even make a big difference in the world.

Activity F–Write the following quote on the board;

"A wise man makes his own decisions, an ignorant man follows public opinion."-Chinese proverb

Have the class copy the quote into their journals. Then lead a discussion about the quote and its meaning.

Activity G–Spotlight

Collect all of the journals. Pick one journal without letting the students see which one you pick. Read the answers to the Spotlight questions in that journal and see if someone can guess whose answers you've read. You can either have the students stand and then sit when an answer is not theirs, leaving the last person standing. Or you can read the answers and at the end choose a student to guess. After the person is guessed, ask them to come to the front of the class. Ask them more questions about themselves such as pets, siblings, hobbies, etc. Next ask members of the class to say 5 nice things about this person being Spotlighted. While they are doing this write the name of the student being

3

Spotlighted in the center of a piece of construction paper. Pass around the sheet and let all students write something positive about that person all over the page. When the paper is done being passed around to each student, you will collect it and give it to the student.

Make sure all of the comments are positive before handing back to the student. Also write the word "Done" on the front of the journals of those you have Spotlighted so you don't repeat! You will Spotlight about 3-4 students during each lesson depending on how many there are in the class.

Tell the class that these Spotlight papers are for them to keep in a safe place. If they are having a bad day and not feeling good about themselves, then they can get out this paper and see the positive comments that were made about them. This should raise their self-esteem!

Summarize the lesson by asking the students the following question; "Who has the greatest opportunity to compliment you?" They might say things like their parents, teachers, or friends. The correct answer is themselves! Teach them that no matter what anyone else says about them, they have the choice to believe the positives rather than the negatives. They need to use their wisdom to know that they always have the choice to have good self-esteem.

<u>Silhouette for Chalkboard Activity</u>

1. Cut out outline of head
2. Write your name at the bottom (at neck)
3. Write what "You Know" in the center.

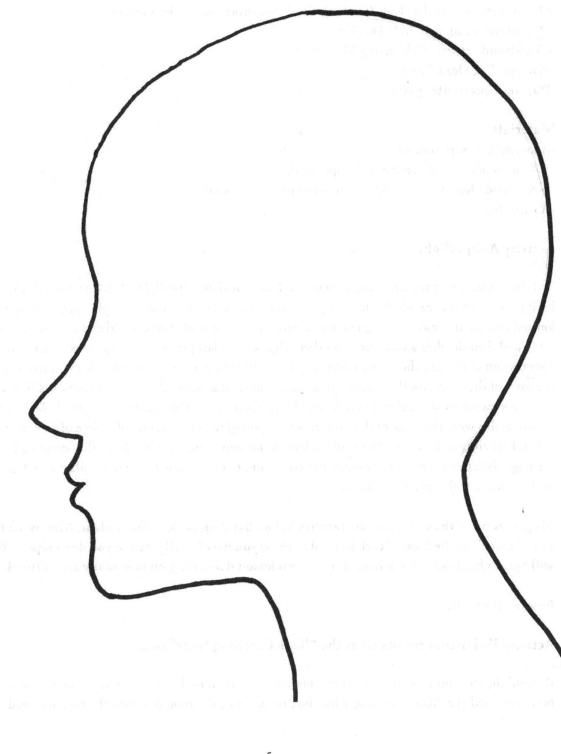

INDVIDUALITY

Objectives
-Spotlight
-Discuss results from the "Kids Catching Kids" box (from the previous lesson)
-Discuss the meaning of individuality
-Chalkboard activity "Celebrating Me Graph"
-Play the "Bag Heads" game
-Play the "Special Me" game

Materials
-A journal for every student
-3-4 pieces of construction paper for Spotlights
-Box labeled "Kids Catching Kids" (from the previous lesson)
-A paper bag

Activity A–Spotlight

Tell the students that you are going to start the lesson by doing Spotlight. Pick one journal without letting the students see which one you pick. Read the answers to the Spotlight questions in that journal and see if someone can guess whose answers you've read. You can either have the students stand and then sit when an answer is not theirs, leaving the last person standing, or you can read the answers and at the end choose a student to guess. After the person is guessed, ask them to come to the front of the class. Ask them more questions about themselves such as pets, siblings, hobbies, etc. Next, ask members of the class to say 5 nice things about this person being Spotlighted. While they are doing this write the name of the student being Spotlighted in the center of a piece of construction paper. Pass around the sheet and let all students write something positive about that person all over the page. When the paper is done being passed around to each student, you will collect it and give it to the student at the end of the lesson.

Make sure all of the comments are positive before handing back to the student. Also, write the word "Done" on the front of each journal of those you have Spotlighted so you don't repeat. You will Spotlight about 3-4 students during each lesson depending on how many are in the class.

Pass out journals.

Activity B–Discuss results from the "Kids Catching Kids" box

Remind the students that wisdom is knowing what you need to do and choosing to do it. Ask them how they used the "Kids Catching Kids" box throughout the month. Open the box and read the notes to see the smart decisions that they made. Have a discussion about their choices and how they made a difference.

Activity C–Discuss the meaning of Individuality

Tell students that today you are going to talk about individuality. Ask them if they know the meaning. Then write the word on the board. **Individuality is discovering who you are meant to be so you can make a difference.** Have them write the definition in their journals. Read the following; individuality is important because it builds confidence and emphasizes a child's uniqueness. What if we all looked alike, dressed the same, and did everything just like everyone else? Wouldn't that be boring? Fortunately we are all different. Think about all of the different people in our school. Did you know that every single person in this school is different and unique? Each person here is special in some way. Today I hope you will find a way to meet a student at our school whom you've never met or talked to before. Say "hi", and then find out what makes them unique. You will surely learn a lot from others and yourself and be better for it.

Activity D–Chalkboard activity "Celebrating Me Graph"

On the chalkboard write the words "Everybody is Different". Then tell the students that they are going to help you make a graph. Have them collect genetic information about themselves and then graph it under the words "Everybody is Different".

Here are some ideas:

-Which students have curly hair? Straight hair?
-How many can curl their tongues?
-How many can wiggles their ears?
-How many have dimples?
-How many students have blue eyes? Brown eyes? Green eyes?

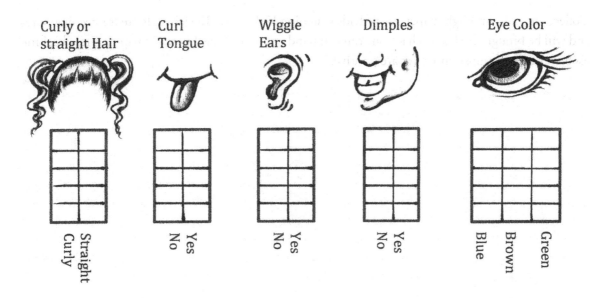

Graph the information and lead a discussion with the class on how they are different and how they are alike. Encourage the students to celebrate their diversity. Help them understand that all of their genetic traits are unique and special.

Activity E–Play the "Bag Heads" game

Put a paper bag over a child's head. Everyone else walks around the room until the "bag head" says "freeze"! Everyone stays where they are while the "bag head" wanders around trying to find someone. When they do, they should try to guess who the student is by touching above the shoulders. If the guess is correct, the person identified gets to wear the bag. Allow 4-5 students to take a turn or as long as the time permits. This game teaches that we are all unique physically and uses our different senses besides sight in recognizing others differences.

Activity F–Play the "Special Me" game

Ask the students to tear out a sheet of paper from their journals. Have them write their name on one side. Collect all of the papers. Then mix them up and pass out to the students making sure no one gets their own name. Tell them that they are going to look at the name on the paper and write on the back a compliment about that person. An example might be, a glorious mane of hair, the cleanest fingernails, the best dressed of the day, or any personal quality, however profound or whimsical.

Then put all of the papers into a basket or hat. Take out the papers and read the compliments. Have the students try and guess who the person is who you are reading about. This game should make the students feel better about themselves when they hear what has been said about them. This should be fun!

Summarize the lesson by asking the students this question, "If you feel you look different than everyone around you, does that lower your self esteem?" Tell them that they should be proud of being different. Everyone has different qualities and talents that make them unique and help add variety to the world we live in. If we were all the same, the world would be a pretty boring place.

Collect journals, Spotlight papers, and "Kids Catching Kids" box. The journals are for keeping notes and will be brought back at each lesson. You can hand out each of the Spotlight papers after checking each comment to make sure they are positive.

COOPERATION

Objectives
-Spotlight
-Discuss the meaning of cooperation
-Art activity to illustrate cooperation
-Discuss lessons from nature by reading facts about ants
-Puzzle
-Activity "Pulling Together"

Materials
-A journal for every student
-3-4 pieces of construction paper for Spotlights
-Puzzle – any puzzle with 8-12 preferably large pieces
-A yard stick, 4 pieces of string, each cut 2 yards long, a small piece of paper with the words "Family Unity" written on it.

Activity A–Spotlight

Tell the students that you are going to start the lesson by doing Spotlight. Pick one journal without letting the students see which one you pick. Read the answers to the Spotlight questions in that journal and see if someone can guess whose answers you've read. You can either have the students stand and then sit when an answer is not theirs, leaving the last person standing, or you can read the answers and at the end choose a student to guess. After the person is guessed, ask them to come to the front of the class. Ask them more questions about themselves such as pets, siblings, hobbies, etc. Next, ask members of the class to say 5 nice things about this person being Spotlighted. While they are doing this write the name of the student being Spotlighted in the center of a piece of construction paper. Pass around the sheet and let all students write something positive about that person all over the page. When the paper is done being passed around to each student, you will collect it and give it to the student at the end of the lesson.

Make sure all comments are positive before handing back to the student. Also, write the word "Done" on the front of each journal of those you have Spotlighted so you don't repeat. You will Spotlight about 3-4 students during each lesson depending on how many are in the class

Pass out all journals.

Activity B–Discuss the meaning of Cooperation

Tell the students that today you are going to talk about cooperation. Write the word on the board. Ask them if they know the definition. As a class, "spider web" the word cooperation. This is done by having the students give you ideas about cooperation, then drawing lines from the word to their statements. Have the students write the definition of cooperation in their journals. **Cooperation is working together to do more than you can do alone.** Ask them to think about all of the ways someone may have already cooperated with them today. Did someone help them get breakfast? Did someone help them get to school? Will someone help them learn something new today? Tell them that all day long they will be cooperating with others so that they can do more than they could do alone. Ask the students some things that they can help someone else do by cooperating.

Activity C–Art activity to illustrate cooperation

Tell the students to turn to a new page in their journals. Discuss how the two matching letters in the word "cooperation" remind us of what it means to cooperate. (The two O's work together). Have the students come up with more creative ways of showing how two circles work together, or cooperate with each other, to form something important that we need. (For example the number 8, eyeglasses, tires on a car, etc.). After they are done drawing in their journals have them turn the paper over and list ways they can show cooperation throughout a normal school day. (Walking in a line, waiting their turn or holding the door open for others, etc.). Ask the students to imagine how the day would look if no one showed cooperation with each other. Would they be frustrated, irritated or confused? Let the students make facial expressions to show how they would feel.

Activity D–Discuss lessons from nature by reading about ants

It doesn't take very long for a group of ants to find your picnic lunch. News travels fast in an ant colony. This is one reason scientists call ants one of the most cooperative species of all insects. People talk by speaking, but ants talk by smelling. When an ant finds something good to eat, it hurries back to the colony leaving behind a special trail. Soon hundreds of ants find their way back to the food by following its trail. Ants can lift fifty times their weight. That is like a person lifting two small cars at the same time. The ant lives an average of 8 years. Ants live in colonies which are made up of thousands of ants that live and work together. They are called social insects because different ants in the colony do different things to help in the work of the colony. In every ant colony, there is usually one Queen, thousands of workers, soldiers or other specialized groups all working together. Have the students journal some of the interesting ant facts in regard to cooperation.

Activity E–Puzzle activity

Tell the class that you have a puzzle that you want them to put together. Pick as many students as you have pieces to come up to the front of the class to put the puzzle together. Give each student a piece and only one minute to finish the puzzle. When they are finished, have the rest of the class tell you if they cooperated well or not in finishing the task in a short amount of time. This is an interesting activity, as it demonstrates how well the students are capable of working with each other.

Activity F–"Pulling together"

Print the words "Family Unity" on a small piece of paper and tape it to the top of a yard stick. Cut 4 pieces of string 2 yards long, and give one string to four different students. Explain that the yard stick, string, and sign represent family unity, and that they are going to learn something important about living together as a family from this activity. Have all 4 students surround a desk. Have them tie their string to the yard stick a little above the midway point. Lay the yard stick down in the middle of the desk. Tell them to lay the end of their string down in front of them. Ask one student if he or she can raise the stick to a standing position by pulling the string alone. They will find that one string doesn't support the stick at all. It will fall over easily. Next, ask another student to join the first to see if 2 strings can hold the yard stick up and keep it standing. It may be possible, but the yardstick will be unsteady. Now tell all 4 to pull on their strings and hold the yard stick in an upright position. You may have to slightly adjust the points at which the strings are tied, but with the students pulling from different directions, the yard stick will stand upright. Ask the students what they can learn from this activity. Point out that with everyone "pulling together", your family is able to accomplish more than each person can by themselves. With everyone doing their share, working and playing together as a team, your family will be stronger and happier. Ask them if they can think of times when this has actually been the case. Some examples might be (Cleaning out the garage, yard work, packing the car for a vacation or decorating the Christmas tree). Now have someone pull the yard stick with all of their strength while others pull normally. If one person pulls hard enough, the yard stick will topple over. Ask what this shows about family unity. If someone is selfish or controlling, they can destroy the balance and soon spoil the family's feelings of cooperation and togetherness.

Summarize the lesson by telling the students that whether cleaning, folding laundry, or finishing a science project, it is more fun to work with someone than it is to work alone. Tell them that today you hope that they will thank all of the people who cooperate with them to get the big things done. Give a hug, make a card, or write a letter to say thank you to at least one person who cooperated with you today.

Collect all journals and Spotlight papers from the students. You can hand back each of the Spotlight papers after you have checked to make sure all of the comments are positive.

COMPASSION

Objectives
-Spotlight
-Discuss the meaning of compassion
-Draw ways to be compassionate and make "Compassion Cards"
-Read story about Orca whales
-Act out compassion skit and discuss situation cards
-Play the "Let me help you" game

Materials
-A journal for every student
-3-4 pieces of construction paper for Spotlights
-A piece of paper for every student
-Situation cards – (3-3X5 cards with scenarios listed in lesson)
-A blindfold
-Quotes

Activity A–Spotlight

Tell the students that you are going to start the lesson by doing Spotlight. Pick one journal without letting the students see which one you pick. Read the answers to the Spotlight questions in that journal and see if someone can guess whose answers you've read. You can either have the students stand and then sit when an answer is not theirs, leaving the last person standing, or you can read the answers and at the end choose a student to guess. After the person is guessed, ask them to come to the front of the class. Ask them more questions about themselves such as pets, siblings, hobbies, etc. Next, ask members of the class to say 5 nice things about this person being Spotlighted. While they are doing this write the name of the student being Spotlighted in the center of a piece of construction paper. Pass around the sheet and let all students write something positive about that person all over the page. When the paper is done being passed around to each student, you will collect it and give it to the student at the end of the lesson.

Make sure all of the comments are positive before handing back to the student. Also, write the word "Done" on the front of each journal of those you have Spotlighted so you don't repeat. You will Spotlight about 3-4 students during each lesson depending on how many are in the class.

Pass out the remaining journals.

Activity B–Discuss the meaning of compassion

Tell the students that this month they are going to learn about compassion. Ask them if they know the meaning of the word. Have them write in their journals the definition. **Compassion is caring enough to do something about someone else's need.** Tell them to think for a moment about some of the needs people have.

Everyone has a need for food, clothing, a place to live, love and friendship. Have you ever considered using your time and the things you own to meet someone else's needs? Today, think about your free time. How could you use your free time to meet someone else's needs? Compassion also means that you are being sensitive to the needs of others and always looking for a way to help them. Ask the students to share a time when someone showed compassion towards them. Then ask them how it made them feel.

Activity C–Draw ways to be compassionate and make "Compassion Cards"

Have the students draw in their journals a picture of how they can show compassion to someone in need. Give them a few minutes to do this. Have volunteers show the class their drawings. Next, pass out a sheet of paper to each student. Using crayons or marker, have each student make a "Compassion Card" for someone who may need it. Cards may say, "I'm thinking of you in your time of need", "I love you because….." or "Thank you for…."

Activity D–Read story about Orca whales

Did you know that an Orca whale can weigh as much as 18,000 pounds? They can grow up to 35 feet long, live to be 75 years old, and travel at speeds of 30 mph in the ocean. Orca whales are very smart and easy to train. They love to be petted and like to please their trainers. Sometimes they even make up their own tricks and teach them to their trainers. One important way that Orca whales prove how smart they are is the way they show compassion for other Orcas. When one Orca whale calls for help, members of their family can tell they are in trouble and will quickly come to help. Even if it means risking their own life, Orcas will help any other Orca that is in trouble. When a whale becomes sick and has trouble breathing, one or two other whales will lift it to the surface so that it won't drown. Sometimes whales get beached or stuck where the water is too shallow, trying to help another whale. Scientists believe that these whales have strong social ties because of the way they communicate and care for each other. Although they are strong and fierce mammals, Orca whales seem to care enough to help their friends when they have a problem.

Activity E–Act out compassion skit and discuss situation cards

Pick three students from the class to act out a skit. Tell two of the students that they are playing on the playground, and the third student is new to the class and sitting alone on the playground. How could the two students show compassion for the new student? After the skit, discuss with the class why it is important to show compassion to a new student.

Next pass out the situation cards that were made for this lesson. The cards are made using 3-3X5 cards and writing one situation on each card. The situations are listed below. Have the students comment on each.

1. Once I helped a friend by…
2. When someone is sick, I can…
3. Once someone showed compassion for me by…

Activity F–Play the "Let me help you" game

Create an obstacle course that isn't too difficult. You may use chairs, books or trash cans. Pick two students to be partners. One person wears a blindfold and the other is a helper. Start by having the blindfolded player try to navigate through the obstacles without any help. They may refuse or may try and laugh, trip or fall. Next, have the helper guide the blindfolded player through the course. Let other students have a turn so that they can have a chance to experience how good it feels to give and receive help.

Display the following quotes and have the students write them in their journals.

1. "To ease another's heartache is to forget one's own". Abraham Lincoln
2. "Be the change you want to see in the world". Mahatma Ghandi
3. "If you can't feed a hundred people, then just feed one". Mother Teresa

Summarize the lesson by telling the students that reaching out to others makes life meaningful. What is really great about this is that the more you give, the more you will receive. You will be happier in life. And you will have even greater self-esteem.

Collect all journals and Spotlight papers from the students. You can hand back each of the Spotlight papers after you have checked to make sure all of the comments are positive.

SELF-DISCIPLINE

Objectives
-Spotlight
-Discuss the meaning of Self-Discipline
-Pose scenarios of Self-Discipline and discuss worksheet
-Read story about Squirrels
-"Goalies" object lesson
-Discuss ways to deal with anger

Materials
-A journal for every student
-3-4 pieces of construction paper for Spotlights
-Self-Discipline worksheet for every student
-A handful of pennies or other coins

Activity A–Spotlight

Tell the students that you are going to start the lesson by doing Spotlight. Pick one journal without letting the students see which one you pick. Read the answers to the Spotlight questions in that journal and see if someone can guess whose answers you've read. You can either have the students stand and then sit when an answer is not theirs, leaving the last person standing, or you can read the answers and at the end choose a student to guess. After the person is guessed, ask them to come to the front of the class. Ask them more questions about themselves such as pets, siblings, hobbies, etc. Next, ask members of the class to say 5 nice things about this person being Spotlighted. While they are doing this write the name of the student being Spotlighted in the center of a piece of construction paper. Pass around the sheet and let all students write something positive about that person all over the page. When the paper is done being passed around to each student, you will collect it and give it to the student at the end of the lesson.

Make Sure all of the comments are positive before handing back to the student. Also, write the word "Done" on the front of each journal so you know only to Spotlight each student once. You will Spotlight about 3-4 students during each lesson depending on how many are in the class.

Pass out the remaining journals.

Activity B–Discuss the meaning of Self-Discipline

Tell the students that today you are going to talk about self-discipline. Ask them if they know the definition of the word. Write on the board, **self-discipline is the ability to be in control of your actions so you can make good choices.** Have them write this definition in their journals. Tell them that self-discipline is required to accomplish any task. Completing projects on time or just being consistent with their daily routine requires self-discipline. Point to self-discipline on the board and ask a student to identify how many "I"s and "U"s there are in the word. After they see there are only "I"s and no "U"s, tell them that having self discipline involves "I" not "U". It is something "I" should choose to do, and not expect "U" to do for me. Have the students write three statements in their journals that begin with "I". For example, "I will take care of my things" or "I will listen to my teacher". Encourage students to share their statements with the class.

Talk about how being self-disciplined means doing what is needed, even if you don't feel like it at the time. Write on the board these three sentences, and have the students fill in the blanks. "_____ needed to be done. Instead I wanted to _____. But I choose to be self-disciplined and _____ happened." Steer the students toward the topics of homework and chores to make this more interesting.

Activity C–Pose scenarios of self-discipline and discuss worksheet

Pose the following scenarios to the class. Ask students to give a "thumbs up" or "thumbs down" to show whether they have enough self-discipline to accomplish the named task.

1. Run a mile without stopping.
2. Choose to eat carrot sticks instead of potato chips at lunch.
3. Turn off the computer game before it is over and go to bed.
4. Choose not to hit their sibling back after he or she hits them first.
5. Finish a project and turn it in before it is due.

Ask, "Why is it so hard to have self-discipline? How could you be more successful if you showed more self-discipline in your life?"

Pass out self-discipline worksheet and explain directions. Give the students a few minutes to do the worksheet, then discuss their responses.

Activity D–Read story about Squirrels.

Walking through a forest, the familiar sounds of chattering, scampering and occasional dropping of nuts or pine cones are reminders that the lively squirrels are busy working and playing in the trees overhead. High in the treetops, these furry little animals work constantly during the fall to build up stores of food for the barren months ahead. At a glance, squirrels may appear playful and carefree, but storing large quantities of food for the coming winter is serious business. They work from dawn until dusk for nearly three months, harvesting, eating and storing. This activity requires a tremendous amount of discipline because squirrels are truly playful by nature.

Squirrels are fascinating to watch as they run along the ground with a nut in their mouth searching for the perfect place to bury their prize. Once the spot is found, they use their front feet to dig a couple of inches into the ground. Then the seed is dropped in the hole and covered with leaves and dirt. Finally, the squirrel pats down everything with it's feet, all in about one minutes time. Squirrels store so many nuts that some are never recovered and many sprout into new trees. Providing for their needs in the winter also helps to grow new forests. The squirrel's discipline to do what needs to be done benefits others, as well as themselves.

Activity E–"Goalies" object lesson

Explain to the students that they should all have goals in their lives. Goals can be small or big, short term or long term. To accomplish any goal, a person needs self-discipline. Choose one student from the class to come up front. Put some coins in your hand. Show the student the coins and tell them that these are special coins called "Goalies". Stand a few feet away from the student and ask them if they can catch the "Goalies" when you toss them. Then toss the handful of coins to them. Naturally they will go all over the place, and the student will probably only catch 1 or 2. Now try it again, except now toss just one coin at a time to the student. They should be able to catch them. Explain that the reason these coins are called "Goalies" is that they are like goals. When we try to work on too many goals at the same time, it can be difficult, and most of the goals won't be accomplished. When we catch one at a time, we have more success. Ask the students to share some of their goals and how they used self-discipline to accomplish them.

Activity F–Discuss ways to deal with anger

Ask the students, do you get in a lot of fights? Do other kids pick fights with you? Are you often mad at someone? Do some kids act like they are afraid of you? If you said yes to any of these questions, you might need to learn how to handle your anger. We all get angry sometimes and that is okay. But it is not okay to hit, fight, yell, or name-call when you are mad about something. There are lots of ways to let angry feelings out, and to deal with problems that upset you. To do this, you can learn steps from being CALM. (Write the word on the board.) Have the students copy the following in their journals.

CALM stands for the first word of each step. Calm, Admit, Learn, and Make.

Calm yourself down. There are lots of ways to do this. Take a deep breath, speak slowly, or soften your voice. You might even take the time to do something else such as rest, read or exercise.

Admit that you have a problem. Look at what happened and what you said or did. "I yelled." "I said something mean." "I broke the light." Don't run away or ignore it. It's okay to make mistakes if you learn from them.

Learn to share your feelings with someone. Talk about angry or upset feelings with an adult you trust. Have the person help you find ways to deal with angry feelings.

Make a change in how you deal with anger. Decide on something safe and healthy to do when you feel angry. Is it safe to throw things, holler at people, or hit or kick people? What can you do instead? Decide that the next time you are angry and having a conflict, you'll count to ten backwards before you speak, think of something nice to say, or walk away until you feel better.

Summarize the lesson by saying sometimes self-discipline takes a lot of work to control ourselves and to get things done. You will always feel better about yourself if you practice good self-discipline.

Collect all journals and Spotlight papers from the students. You can hand back each of the Spotlight papers after you have checked to make sure all of the comments are positive.

Self-discipline worksheet

Directions: Circle the things you can do that show you have respect for yourself.

Eat good food

Watch TV or videos all day

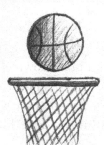
Read

Play computer games all day

Make things

Play sports

Play games with friends

Eat only cookies for lunch

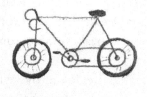
Ride a bike

H O N E S T Y

Objectives
-Spotlight
-Discuss the meaning of honesty
-Play Two Truths and a Lie
-Read story about Goose
-Scenarios on Honesty

Materials
-A journal for every student
-Construction paper for 2-3 Spotlights

Activity A–Spotlight

Tell the students that you are going to start the lesson by doing Spotlight. Pick one journal without letting the students see which one you pick. Read the answers to the Spotlight questions in that journal and see if someone can guess whose answers you've read. You can either have the students stand and then sit when an answer is not theirs, leaving the last person standing, or you can read the answers and at the end choose a student to guess. After the person is guessed, ask them to come to the front of the class. Ask them more questions about themselves such as pets, siblings, hobbies, etc. Next, ask members of the class to say 5 nice things about this person being Spotlighted. While they are doing this write the name of the student being Spotlighted in the center of a piece of construction paper. Pass around the sheet and let all students write something positive about that person all over the page. When the paper is done being passed around to each student, you will collect it and give it to the student at the end of the lesson.

Make sure all of the comments are positive before handing back to the students. Also, write the word "Done" on the front of each journal of those you have Spotlighted so you don't repeat. You will Spotlight about 3-4 students during each lesson depending on how many are in the class.

Pass out the remaining journals.

Activity B–Discuss the meaning of Honesty

Ask the students if they know what honesty means. Have them write in their journals the definition as you write it on the chalkboard. **Honesty is watching what you say and do so others will trust you.** Discuss why honesty is necessary if you are learning to trust and be trusted. It requires an accurate reporting of the facts and telling others what they need to hear. Ask the students what Honesty means to them, and if it is always easy to be honest. Ask if there is a time when you think it is okay not to be honest. Ask them if they want others to be honest with them and why. Lead a discussion on each

of these topics. And lastly, ask this important question, "What would you do if you were walking in your neighborhood and found a bag with $1000 in it?"

Activity C–Play Two Truths and a Lie

Ask the students to write down three sentences on a page in their journals and number each sentence. Two of these sentences should be something true about them, and one of the sentences should be a lie. Some of the statements could be about where they live, where they were born, their favorite book, etc. Instruct them to write their name on the back of their paper. Instruct the students to rip out this page and collect them from each student.

Read them and see if the students can identify the one lie in each page.

Activity D–Read the story about Goose

Sometimes when you look up at the sky, you can see birds flying in the shape of a "V". It is the way geese travel when they are going south for the winter. A Canadian goose can grow up to be 4 feet tall with wings that stretch out as far as 6 feet. The goose that lies in front cuts through the wind so flying can be easier for the rest of the geese. By following the lead goose, the rest of the flock can reach their destination faster and with fewer stops along the way. When the bird in front gets tired, it moves to the back of the flock and another bird takes its place. Geese have to learn to trust each other. Those who lead have to go the right direction, and those who follow have to know they can depend on the actions of the goose that is leading. Honesty works a lot like a lead goose. When you are honest, it helps others trust you. When you are careful about what you say and do, everyone around you will learn to trust you and you will learn to trust them.

Activity E–Scenarios on Honesty

Read the following scenarios and have students respond with correct answers for each.

1. Stephanie went to the grocery store with her mom. While she was at the store, she saw a candy bar that she really wanted. She didn't have any money. She put the candy bar in her pocket anyway. Was this honest? What should she do?
2. Jason wanted to go to the school football game with his friends. His mom said he couldn't go to the game, but had to go to a church activity instead. Jason agreed, but when he left the house, he went to the football game instead. Was this honest? What should Jason do?
3. Megan was having a hard time in her math class at school. The final exam was coming quickly and she hadn't studied for it. Her best friend, Lisa, said that she could look at her answers during the test. Is Megan being honest? Is Lisa being honest? What should they do?
4. Amy told her best friend, Melissa, a personal secret. Melissa promised not to tell anyone. When Amy wasn't around, Melissa told Amy's secret to others. Was this honest? What should Melissa do?

Summarize the lesson by reminding the students that they should strive to be honest with themselves and everyone around them. When they are honest it will raise their self-esteem.

Collect all journals and Spotlight papers from the students. You can hand back each of the Spotlight papers after you have checked to make sure all of the comments are positive.

GRATITUDE

Objectives
-Spotlight
-Discuss the meaning of Gratitude
-Make Gratitude List
-Gratitude Riddle
-Pebble in the Shoe
-Gratitude Letters

Materials
-A journal for every student
-Construction paper for 3-4 Spotlights
-1 small pebble (rock) and a piece of candy
-1 piece of paper for each student

Activity A–Spotlight

Tell the students that you are going to start the lesson by doing Spotlight. Pick one journal without letting the students see which one you pick. Read the answers to the Spotlight questions in that journal and see if someone can guess whose answers you've read. You can either have the students stand and then sit when an answer is not theirs, leaving the last person standing, or you can read the answers and at the end choose a student to guess. After the person is guessed, ask them to come to the front of the class. Ask them more questions about themselves such as pets, siblings, hobbies, etc. Next, ask members of the class to say 5 nice things about this person being Spotlighted. While they are doing this write the name of the student being Spotlighted in the center of a piece of construction paper. Pass around the sheet and let all students write something positive about that person all over the page. When the paper is done being passed around to each student, you will collect it and give it to the student at the end of the lesson.

Make sure all of the comments are positive before handing back to the student. Also, write the word "Done" on the front of each journal of those you have Spotlighted so you don't repeat. You will Spotlight about 3-4 students during each lesson depending on how many are in the class.

Pass out all journals

Activity B–Discuss the meaning of Gratitude

Tell the students that today you are going to be talking about Gratitude. Write the word on the board and have them write the definition in their journals. **Gratitude is saying thank you for something you have received.** Discuss why saying thank you is a very important action. When thanks is given, both parties are affected in a positive way. When you say thank you to someone who has shown you kindness, it motivates that person to want to do more good deeds. Ask the class if they are good at saying thank you. Ask them how they feel when someone doesn't say thank you when they've done something good for them. Does it make them want to do more or less for that person? Tell them that the more they are grateful for, the more they will be likely to receive.

Activity C–Make a Gratitude List

Have the students write in their journals 10 things that they are grateful for and why. An example of something they might be grateful for could be their teacher, because of all the time they spend in preparation for their instruction. Have a few students share some of their answers.

Activity D–Gratitude Riddle

Tell the students that you have some riddles for them. Say each one of the riddles out loud, giving one clue at a time, and ask the students for their guesses. Limit one guess after each clue that is given to help with the time.

Riddle 1:
-I am something everyone needs.
-I am in every land in the world.
-I help things grow.
-I am used for bathing and swimming
-I am delicious when you are thirsty.
What am I? WATER

Riddle 2:
-I am liked by people everywhere.
-I can help you grow.
-Animals of all kinds need me also.
-I come in all colors, shapes and sizes.
-I taste like many different things.
What am I? FOOD

Riddle 3:
-I am something people live in.
-I am made of wood, bricks, stone and even snow.
-People are happy to live inside me.
-I keep you warm, dry and protected.
What am I? A HOME

Riddle 4:
-I bring happiness to others.
-I make the world warm and bright.
-I am high in the sky.
-I am big and round.
-You see me more in the summer than in the winter.

What am I? THE SUN

Riddle 5:
-I am usually green.
-I grow on the ground.
-Children like to play on me.
-People have picnics on me.
-Fathers mow me when I grow too long.
What am I? THE GRASS

Riddle 6:
-I can be different colors.
-I keep you warm.
-I should be worn or hung up.
-Sometimes you button or zip me.
-I need to be washed when I get dirty.
What am I? CLOTHES

Activity E–Pebble in the shoe

Pick a student to come to the front of the room. Have them take off one shoe and put a small pebble inside of their shoe. Have the student then put their shoe back on. Then give them a piece of candy to eat immediately. With the pebble in their shoe, and candy in their mouth, have them walk around the room. When they are finished, ask them which experience they noticed more. Would the candy have been more enjoyable to eat without the pebble as a distraction? Explain that when we are ungrateful and complain, it is like we have a pebble in our shoe. We don't fully experience all our blessings, and we don't notice them as easily.

Activity F–Gratitude Letters

Pass out a piece of paper to each student. Tell them that you want them to write a letter to someone who they appreciate and tell them why. These letters can be given out whenever the students choose to deliver them to the person to whom they wrote.

End the lesson by asking 3 different students the following questions.

1. What was a great experience that happened to you?
2. What is a talent or special gift you are grateful to have?
3. What is a quality you admire in the person sitting next to you?

When you are finished, tell the class that each of these students, by being aware of what they are grateful for, have all raised their self-esteem.

Collect all journals and Spotlight papers from the students. Pass out each of the Spotlight papers after you have checked to make sure all of the comments are positive.

FORGIVENESS

Objectives
-Finish Spotlights
-Discuss the meaning of Forgiveness
-Object lesson on Forgiveness
-Final review of Project Self Esteem

Materials
-A journal for every student
-Enough construction paper to finish Spotlights
-1 clear glass, vinegar, bleach, water, food coloring
-Prizes

Activity A–Spotlight

Tell the students that you are going to start the lesson by doing Spotlight. Pick one journal without letting the students see which one you pick. Read the answers to the Spotlight questions in that journal and see if someone can guess whose answers you've read. You can either have the students stand and then sit when an answer is not theirs, leaving the last person standing, or you can read the answers and at the end choose a student to guess. After the person is guessed, ask them to come to the front of the class. Ask them more questions about themselves such as pets, siblings, hobbies, etc. Next, ask members of the class to say 5 nice things about this person being Spotlighted. While they are doing this write the name of the student being Spotlighted in the center of a piece of construction paper. Pass around the sheet and let all students write something positive about that person all over the page. When the paper is done being passed around to each student, you will collect it and give it to the student at the end of the lesson. **Finish all Spotlights since this is the last lesson.**

Pass out the remaining journals.

Activity B–Discuss the meaning of Forgiveness

Tell the class that today you are going to discuss the meaning of Forgiveness. Have them open their journals and write the following definition. **Forgiveness is deciding that someone who has wronged you doesn't have to pay.** Tell them that there are 4 basic steps to have forgiveness.

1. Be Sympathetic and listen with an open heart.
2. Bring both people together to see the problem from both sides.
3. Talk to the person who has hurt you because usually problems can be solved here with it being a simple misunderstanding.
4. Be patient and let each person talk without interruption.

The students must realize that forgiving someone may not take the hurt away, it just starts the healing process. Also, discuss why it is a good thing to show forgiveness. Have the students take out a piece of paper from their journals. Ask them to write about a time when someone wronged them. Ask them not to put their name on it. Collect all papers and choose several to read aloud and have the students brainstorm ways they can show forgiveness in each situation. Then ask the students what it would be like if no one in the world showed forgiveness.

Activity C–Object lesson on Forgiveness

Show the students a clear glass. Pour a mixture of half water and half vinegar into the glass. Tell the class that the glass represents a boy named Warren. Tell the class that you are going to tell them a story about Warren. Warren was a young boy who always seemed to get into trouble. One day he was walking to school and throwing rocks along the way when he accidentally broke a house window. He ran to school and never told anyone about it. (Add a drop of food coloring to the glass). Continue the story adding several more instances of Warren getting into trouble and lying about it, such as stealing money or cheating on a test, etc. As you relate the story, add a drop of food coloring to Warren's glass each time he does something wrong. Point out that the first time Warren did something wrong, the color didn't affect too much of the water. But each additional time he did something wrong, "He" became darker and cloudier. The stain had finally permeated his entire being and filled him with guilt. Eventually Warren felt miserable. His friends didn't want to be around him because he was always getting into trouble, and they couldn't trust him. He didn't like the way his life was going or the way he felt so he decided to talk with the Principal and his parents because he wanted to change his ways. Together they helped him come up with a plan. First he went to the neighbor and apologized for the broken window and offered to pay for the damages. Then he went and confessed his other wrong doings. As you tell this part of the story with examples of how Warren has asked for forgiveness, add a drop of bleach with each example. Eventually the glass will become clear again. Ask the class how they think Warren feels about himself now that he has asked for forgiveness. Ask them if they know the steps they need to go through to make amends for an act of dishonesty.

1. Recognize they have done something wrong.
2. Apologize to the person they have offended.
3. Repair the relationship.
4. Resolve not to do it again.

Summarize the lesson by telling the students that their self-esteem will be better if they will ask for forgiveness when they have wronged another. It is just as important to forgive others and not hold grudges.

Activity D–Final review of Project Self Esteem

Before the lesson, read through the previous lessons from this past year and write down some questions to ask the class about the subjects you have taught. Explain that they have used their journals to take notes on the lessons you have taught. They may use their notes to answer your questions. To make it more fun, bring prizes for the students to give when they answer your questions correctly. Prizes could be pencils, stickers, snacks, etc.

End the lesson by telling the students that you have enjoyed helping them learn what good self-esteem means. Tell them that they are the only ones who have the greatest opportunity to compliment themselves. This means that they are the ones who create their own Self-Esteem. No one can ultimately make them believe that they are not good enough. They always have the choice to do better and act better. In turn, they will feel good about themselves.

Pass out Spotlight papers after making sure all comments are positive.

(The journals are for the students to keep.)

WISDOM

Objectives
-Introduce Spotlight –
-Discuss the meaning of wisdom and introduce "Kids Catching Kids" box
-Object lesson "A matter of time"
-Chalkboard activity using Silhouette
-Discuss famous people using wisdom
-Discuss Quotes

Materials
-A journal for every student
-3-4 pieces of construction paper for Spotlights
-Box labeled "Kids Catching Kids"
-Mason Jar (Medium in size)
-1 cup of rice
-8 golf balls
-Silhouette for each student
-Quotes

Activity A–Introduction of facilitator, Project Self Esteem, and Spotlight

Tell the students your name and a little bit about yourself. Tell them that you are here to teach Project Self-Esteem. Self-esteem is how you feel about yourself. If you feel good about yourself, you will be happy and treat others well. Explain that your goal is to teach them to have good self-esteem through your lessons each month. Tell them that each one of them is special and this year you are going to find out why.

Pass out a journal to each student and ask them to write their name on the front cover. Tell the students that these journals are for them to take notes in during each of your lessons. Explain that when they take notes they will better remember what you have taught and they will have their notes to refer to at the last lesson where you will have a review of the entire year. Now have the students open to the first page and write the date and number the lines 1 to 10. Ask the 10 following questions;

1. What is your favorite color?
2. What is your favorite food?
3. What is your favorite restaurant?
4. What is your favorite movie or T.V. show?
5. What is your favorite sport?
6. What is your favorite thing to do in your free time?
7. What is a talent that you have?
8. Where is a place that you would like to visit?

9. What would you like to be when you grow up?
10. Who is a person you admire? (dead or alive)

When you are done asking these questions, tell the students that you are going to play a game called Spotlight with them at the end of the lesson. Have them turn to the next page and tell them they will be taking notes throughout the lesson.

Activity B–Introduce the meaning of wisdom and the box labeled "Kids Catching Kids"

Tell the students that today you are going to discuss the meaning of wisdom. Write the word on the board. Ask them if they know the definition. After the discussion, write the definition on the board. **Wisdom is knowing what you need to do and choosing to do it**. Have the students copy this definition into their journal.

Read the following. We know lots of things don't we? We know we should be courteous to others, but sometimes we are not. We know we should be polite and use good manners, but sometimes we don't. We know we should eat things that are good for our bodies, but sometimes we don't. Wisdom is about more than just storing information. It's about more than just learning facts and gaining knowledge. Wisdom is the next step. It is about using what you learn. Wisdom is knowledge being applied to every day life. We can say "I know, I know" to so many things. But until we make the wise choice to apply the things we know, it is just talk isn't it?

Place the box labeled "Kids Catching Kids" where all students can see it. Tell the students that the box will be left in the classroom the entire month to catch students making smart choices. Tell the students that they will be watching for other students making good choices. Then they are to write on a piece of paper the student's name and the good choice they made and place it in the box. (Examples might be, seeing someone picking up trash or being a friend to someone who seems lonely.) Tell the students that next month you will open the box and read the papers to see who has been using their wisdom.

Activity C–"A Matter of Time" (you will need jar, rice, and balls)

Begin by telling the students that the jar represents the amount of time available in 24 hours. Explain that the balls represent all their responsibilities and the "hard things" in their day. (chores, homework, practice, etc.) The rice represents the fun and easy things in their day (playing outdoors, watching TV, etc.) Ask one student to come forward and fill up their day with all of the hard and easy activities. They must fit it all in the jar. They will probably pour rice in first and then add some balls. But unless they put all of the balls in first, they will not be able to fit everything in the jar. Allow them to do it however they think is best. Note that they might not be able to accomplish all that they intended that day. When the student is done, pour everything out, divide the rice and the balls again, and demonstrate the alternative method. This alternative method will allow them to accomplish all their needs and wants in any given time period. Explain that by fulfilling our responsibilities (filling the jar with balls) and tackling some of the hard but important tasks in life first, there will always be time left over for recreation and fun (pouring rice to fill in all of the gaps). When we spend the first part of our day doing easy, unimportant things, it is a form of procrastination, and we are usually too tired or unmotivated to dig into the more challenging activities later in the day. If a student happens to fill up the jar "correctly", point out why it worked and discuss the principles involved.

Activity D–Chalkboard activity using Silhouette

Draw a line down the center of the chalkboard. On the left side, write the title "What I Know". Pass out a silhouette to each student. Have the students write their name at the bottom of the silhouette. Tell each student to write down something that they have learned in the center. (some examples might be; dance, read, play sports, etc.) Collect all of the silhouettes and hang them under the title, "What I Know". Then on the right side of the chalkboard write the title, "What I Do With What I Know". Lead a discussion about how their talents will lead to short and long term goals. (For example; if a student wrote "dance" on their silhouette, then you might write "perform in a recital" under the title "What I do With What I Know".

Activity E–Read about a famous person using wisdom

Martin Luther King Jr. (1929-1968)

Dr. King was the son and grandson of Baptist ministers. At 19 years old, he graduated from Morehouse College. In 1951, he received a Bachelor of Divinity and in 1955 he earned a Ph.D. at Boston University. While in college, he became interested in Mahatma Gandhi and his philosophy of non-violence. In 1954, he became the pastor of a Baptist church in Montgomery, Alabama. In 1955, he became a leader in the Montgomery bus boycott. This is where residents of Montgomery forced the bus company to desegregate its buses. During the early 1960's, Dr. King led many demonstrations throughout the South demanding racial equality and an end to the "Jim Crow" laws which required separate public facilities for blacks and whites. Dr. King was arrested and jailed frequently. In August of 1963, 250,000 people took part in a "March on Washington", the biggest demonstration in U.S. history. It is there where Dr. King gave his famous "I have a dream" speech. In 1964, Dr. King won the Nobel Peace Prize for his works as a leader in the Civil Rights movement. In 1968, while in Memphis to lead a demonstration of striking workers, Dr. King was shot on a hotel balcony.

Lead a discussion on how Martin Luther King was a great example of how someone can use their wisdom to help others and even make a big difference in the world.

Activity F–Write the following quotes on the board;

"A wise man makes his own decisions, an ignorant man follows public opinion."-Chinese proverb
"Live as if you were to die tomorrow. Learn as if you were to live forever."- Mahatma Gandhi

Have the class copy the quotes in their journals. Then lead a discussion about the quotes and their meaning.

Activity G–Spotlight

Collect all of the journals. Pick one journal without letting the students see which one you pick. Read the answers to the Spotlight questions in that journal and see if someone can guess whose answers you've read. You can either have the students stand and then sit when an answer is not theirs, leaving the last person standing. Or you can read the answers and at the end choose a student to guess. After the person is guessed, ask them to come to the front of the class. Ask them more questions about themselves such as pets, siblings, hobbies, etc. Next ask members of the class to say 5 nice things about this person being Spotlighted. While they are doing this write the name of the student being Spotlighted in the center of a piece of construction paper. Pass around the sheet and let all students write something positive about that person all over the page. When the paper is done being passed around to each student, you will collect it and give it to the student.

Make sure all of the comments are positive before handing back to the student. Also, write the word "Done" on the front of each journal of those you have Spotlighted so you don't repeat. You will Spotlight about 3-4 students during each lesson depending on how many students are in the class.

Tell the class that these Spotlight papers are for them to keep in a safe place. If they are having a bad day and not feeling good about themselves, then they can get out this paper and see the positive comments that were made about them. This should raise their self-esteem!

Summarize the lesson by asking the students the following question. "Who has the greatest opportunity to compliment them?" They might say things like their parents, teachers, or friends. It is themselves! Teach them that no matter what anyone else says about them, they have the choice to believe the positives rather than the negatives. They need to use their wisdom to know that they always have the choice to have good self-esteem.

Silhouette for chalkboard activity

1. Cut out outline of head.
2. Write your name at the bottom (at the neck)
3. Write what "you know" in the center

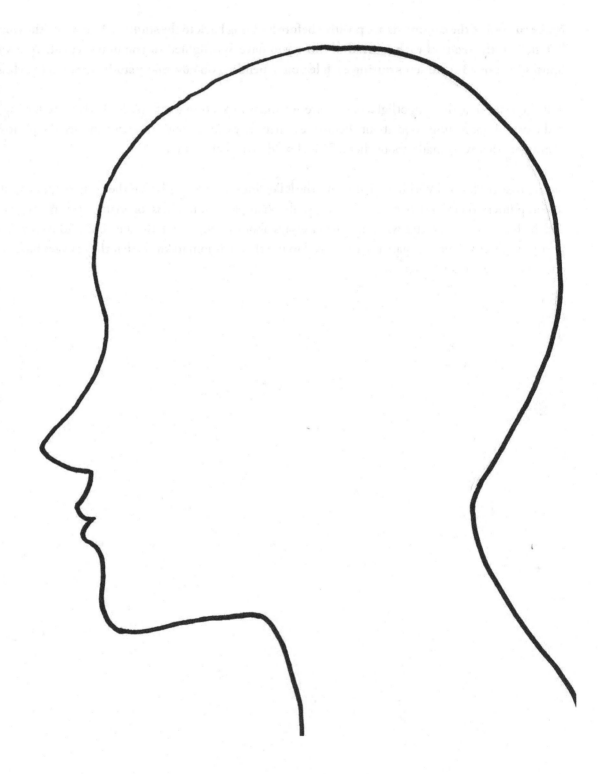

INDIVIDUALITY

Objectives
-Spotlight
-Discuss results from the "Kids Catching Kids" box (from the previous lesson)
-Discuss the meaning of Individuality
-"Preference Profile Sheet" activity
-Play the game, "Special Me"

Materials
-A journal for every student
-3-4 pieces of construction paper for Spotlight
-Box labeled "Kids Catching Kids" (from the previous lesson)
-A copy of the Preference Profile Sheet for every student

Activity A–Spotlight

Tell the students that you are going to start the lesson by doing Spotlight. Pick one journal without letting the students see which one you pick. Read the answers to the Spotlight questions in that journal and see if someone can guess whose answers you've read. You can either have the students stand and then sit when an answer is not theirs, leaving the last person standing, or you can read the answers and at the end choose a student to guess. After the person is guessed, ask them to come to the front of the class. Ask them more questions about themselves such as pets, siblings, hobbies, etc. Next, ask members of the class to say 5 nice things about this person being Spotlighted. While they are doing this write the name of the student being Spotlighted in the center of a piece of construction paper. Pass around the sheet and let all students write something positive about that person all over the page. When the paper is done being passed around to each student, you will collect it and give it to the student at the end of the lesson.

Make sure all of the comments are positive before handing back to the student. Also, write the word "Done" on the front of each journal of those you have Spotlighted so you don't repeat. You will Spotlight about 3-4 students during each lesson depending on how many students that are in the class.

Pass out journals to each student for taking notes.

Activity B–Discuss results from the "Kids Catching Kids" box

Remind the students that wisdom is knowing what you need to do and choosing to do it. Ask them how they used the "Kids Catching Kids" box throughout the month. Open the box and read the notes to see the smart decisions that they made. Have a discussion about their choices and how they made a difference. This should build their self esteem. (Make sure to bring the Wisdom Box back with you after the lesson is over along with other materials)

Activity C–Discuss the meaning of Individuality

Tell students that today you are going to talk about individuality. Ask them if they know the meaning. Then write the word on the board. **Individuality is discovering who you are meant to be so you can make a difference.** Have them write the definition in their journals. Read the following; why is individuality important? Individuality builds confidence and emphasizes a child's uniqueness. What if we all looked alike, dressed the same, and did everything just like everyone else? Wouldn't that be boring? Fortunately we are all different. Think about all of the different people in our school. Did you know that every single person in this school is different and unique? Each person here is special in some way. Today I hope you will find a way to meet a student at our school whom you've never met or talked to before. Say "hi", and then find out what makes them unique. You will surely learn a lot from others and yourself and be better for it.

Activity D–"Preference Profile Sheet" activity

Pass out a copy of the Preference Profile Sheet to each student. Read the Instructions at the top of the page. Give the students a few minutes to answer the questions. This activity will show the students that they have different likes and dislikes. (This should be interesting!) Lead a discussion about these likes and dislikes, and have volunteers give some of their answers. They should also understand that it is OK to be different and that we don't all have to like the same things. It is also important to respect others for being different.

Activity E–Play the game, "Special Me"

Ask the students to tear out a sheet of paper from their journals. Have them write their name on one side. Collect all of the papers. Then mix them up and pass out to the students making sure no one gets their own name. Tell them that they are going to look at the name on the paper and write on the back a compliment about that person. An example might be, a glorious mane of hair, the cleanest fingernails, the best dressed of the day, or any personal quality, however profound or whimsical.

Then put all of the papers into a basket or hat. Take out the papers and read the compliments. Have the students try and guess who the person is that you are reading about. This game should make the students feel better about themselves when they hear what has been said about them. This should be fun!

End the lesson by writing on the board the quote **"We are all something, but none of us is everything"**, by Blaine Pascal. Discuss that we are unique and bring something different to the world. But if we all work together we can make great things happen and in turn will raise our self-esteem.

Collect journals, Spotlight papers and "Kids Catching Kids" box. The journals are for keeping notes and will be brought back at each lesson. You can hand out each of the Spotlight papers after checking each comment to make sure they are positive.

Preference Profile Sheet   Name

Read each of the pairs of statements below and circle the answer that most describes your preference. Please circle one answer in every pair.

If you have difficulty choosing between two answers, circle the answer that is most true for you most of the time.

1. Like to work alone   Like to work with others

2. Morning person   Night person

3. Work by plan   Work in bursts of energy

4. Enjoy routine   Like change

5. Can do several things at once   Need to focus

6. Can see both sides of most issues   Need to take a stand

7. Prefer to eat and sleep on schedule   Eat when hungry/sleep when tired

8. Like music when studying   Prefer quiet when studying

9. Like to work at a desk   Prefer to work on bed or armchair

10. Have a way with animals   Don't care much about animals

11. Like vivid colors   Prefer quiet colors

12. Enjoy a variety of foods   Like to stick with favorite foods

COOPERATION

Objectives

-Spotlight
-Discuss the meaning of Cooperation
-Art activity to illustrate Cooperation
-Discuss lessons from nature by reading facts about Ants
-Rating Cooperation
-Activity "Pulling Together"

Materials

-A journal for every student
-Construction paper for 3-4 Spotlights
-5 pieces of paper with the numbers 1-5, (write one number on each paper)
-Yard stick, 4 pieces of string, each cut 2 yards long, a small piece of paper with the words "Family Unity" written on it.

Activity A–Spotlight

Tell the students that you are going to start the lesson by doing Spotlight. Pick one journal without letting the students see which one you pick. Read the answers to the Spotlight questions in that journal and see if someone can guess whose answers you've read. You can either have the students stand and then sit when an answer is not theirs, leaving the last person standing, or you can read the answers and at the end choose a student to guess. After the person is guessed, ask them to come to the front of the class. Ask them more questions about themselves such as pets, siblings, hobbies, etc. Next, ask members of the class to say 5 nice things about this person being Spotlighted. While they are doing this write the name of the student being Spotlighted in the center of a piece of construction paper. Pass around the sheet and let all students write something positive about that person all over the page. When the paper is done being passed around to each student, you will collect it and give it to the student at the end of the lesson.

Make sure all of the comments are positive before handing back to the student. Also, write the word "Done" on the front of each journal so you know only to Spotlight each student once. You will Spotlight about 3-4 students during each lesson depending on how many students are in the class.

Pass out all journals.

Activity B–Discuss the meaning of Cooperation

Tell the students that today you are going to talk about cooperation. Write the word on the board. Ask them if they know the definition. As a class, "spider web" the word cooperation. This is done by having the students give you ideas about cooperation, then drawing lines from the word to their statements. Have the students write the definition of cooperation in their journals. **Cooperation is working together to do more than you can do alone.** Ask them to think about all of the ways someone may have already cooperated with them today. Did someone help them get breakfast? Did someone help them get to school? Will someone help them learn something new today? Tell them that all day long, they will be cooperating with others so that they can do more than they could do alone. Ask the students some things that they can help someone else do by cooperating.

Activity C–Art activity to illustrate Cooperation

Have the students turn to the next blank page in their journal. Discuss how the two matching letters in the word "Cooperation", remind us of what it means to cooperate. (The two O's work together). Have the students come up with more creative ways of showing how two circles work together, or cooperate with each other, to form something important that we need. (For example the number 8, eye glasses, tires on a car, etc.).

Lead the class in a discussion about what they have learned about cooperation. Do they think it is important to be cooperative? What would the world look like if people were not cooperative?

Activity D–Discuss lessons from nature by reading about ants

It doesn't take very long for a group of ants to find your picnic lunch. News travels fast in an ant colony. This is one reason scientists call ants one of the most cooperative species of all insects. People talk by speaking, but ants talk by smelling. When an ant finds something  good to eat, it hurries back to the colony leaving behind a special trail. Soon hundreds of ants find their way back to the food by following its trail. Ants can lift fifty times their weight. That is like a person lifting two small cars at the same time. The ant lives an average of 8 years. Ants live in colonies which are made up of thousands of ants that live and work together. They are called social insects because different ants in the colony do different things to help in the work of the colony. In every ant colony, there is usually one Queen, thousands of workers, soldiers or other specialized groups all working together. Have the students journal some of the interesting ant facts in regard to cooperation.

Activity E–Rating Cooperation

Write the numbers 1-5 on 5 separate pieces of paper and post on different walls of the classroom. Explain to the students that you are going to give them some scenarios of cooperation. Ask students to rate themselves on a scale of 1-5, with 1 being not very cooperative and 5 being very cooperative. As you mention each scenario, ask students to stand next to the number they would rate themselves. The scenarios are as follows:

1. I listen carefully to others and try to understand what they are saying.
2. I like to share what I have with others.
3. I am happy to volunteer to do something no one else wants to do.
4. I am willing to compromise when I have a disagreement with someone.
5. I try to get along with others when working in a group.

Lead a discussion on each and why some may be more cooperative than others.

Activity F–"Pulling together"

Print the words "Family Unity" on a small piece of paper and tape it to the top of a yard stick. Cut 4 pieces of string 2 yards long, and give one string to four different students. Explain that the yard stick, string, and sign represent family unity, and that they are going to learn something important about living together as a family from this activity. Have all 4 students surround a desk. Have them tie their string to the yard stick a little above the midway point. Lay the yard stick down in the middle of the desk. Tell everyone to lay the end of their string down in front of them. Ask one student if they can raise the stick to a standing position by pulling their string alone. They will find that one string doesn't support the stick at all. It will fall over easily. Next, ask another student to join the first to see if 2 strings can hold the yard stick up and keep it standing. It may be possible, but the yardstick will be unsteady. Now tell all 4 to pull on their strings and hold the yard stick in an upright position. You may have to slightly adjust the points at which the strings are tied, but with the students pulling from different directions, the yard stick will stand upright. Ask the students what they can learn from this activity. Point out that with everyone "pulling together", your family is able to accomplish more than each person can by themselves. With everyone doing their share, working and playing together as a team, your family will be stronger and happier. Ask them if they can think of times when this has actually been the case. (Cleaning out the garage, yard work, packing the car for a vacation or decorating the Christmas tree). Now have someone pull the yard stick with all of their strength while others pull normally. If one person pulls hard enough, the yard stick will topple over. Ask what does this show about family unity. If someone is selfish or controlling, they can destroy the balance and soon spoil the family's feelings of cooperation and togetherness.

Summarize the lesson by telling the students that all of us like it when others help us get big jobs done. Whether it is cleaning our room, folding laundry or finishing a science project, it is more fun to work with someone than it is to work alone. Tell them that today you hope that they will thank all of the people who cooperate with them to get the big things done. Give a hug, make a card, or write a letter to say thank you to at least one person who cooperated with you today.

Collect all journals and Spotlight papers from the students. Pass out Spotlight papers after you have checked to make sure all of the comments are positive.

COMPASSION

Objectives
-Spotlight
-Discuss the meaning of compassion
-Discuss pros and cons of using compassion and discuss situation cards
-Read story about Orca whales
-Make "Compassion Cards"
-Show the "Love Eggs-periment"
-Showing Compassion for Classmates
-Read Poem and discuss quotes

Materials
-A journal for every student
-Construction paper for 3-4 Spotlights
-Situation cards
-A clear drinking glass filled with 1 cup of water
-1 fresh egg
-1/4 cup salt with an extra tablespoon (for measuring)
-Quotes

Activity A–Spotlight

Tell the students that you are going to start the lesson by doing Spotlight. Pick one journal without letting the students see which one you pick. Read the answers to the Spotlight questions in that journal and see if someone can guess whose answers you've read. You can either have the students stand and then sit when an answer is not theirs, leaving the last person standing, or you can read the answers and at the end choose a student to guess. After the person is guessed, ask them to come to the front of the class. Ask them more questions about themselves such as pets, siblings, hobbies, etc. Next, ask members of the class to say 5 nice things about this person being Spotlighted. While they are doing this write the name of the student being Spotlighted in the center of a piece of construction paper. Pass around the sheet and let all students write something positive about that person all over the page. When the paper is done being passed around to each student, you will collect it and give it to the student at the end of the lesson.

Make sure all of the comments are positive before handing back to the students. Also, write the word "Done" on the front of each journal so you know only to Spotlight each student once. You will Spotlight about 3-4 students during each lesson depending on how many are in the class.

Pass out the remaining journals.

Activity B–Discuss the meaning of compassion

Tell the students that this month they are going to learn about compassion. Ask them if they know the meaning of the word. Have them write in their journals the definition. **Compassion is caring enough to do something about someone else's need.** Tell them to think for a moment about some of the needs people have.

Everyone has a need for food, clothing, a place to live, love and friendship. Have you ever considered using your time and the things you own to meet someone else's needs? Today, think about your free time. How could you use your free time to meet someone else's needs?

Tell them the following true story. Benjamin Franklin invented the stove called the Franklin Stove. It is still being made today. At the time, he was offered a patent for his invention. It would have earned him a lot of money. But Franklin refused the patent. Instead, he published a pamphlet describing how to build the stove so blacksmiths or other clever people could make one themselves. You can see how he had compassion for others and was very unselfish.

Activity C–Discuss pros and cons of using compassion and discuss situation cards

Have the class make a list of pros and cons on being compassionate. First, let them name all of the pros they can think of for why they should be compassionate. Write their answers on the board under the heading "Pros". Repeat this process now by allowing the students to list all of cons of being compassionate. When the students have finished, compare the lists and determine which has more items: pros or cons. What does this tell kids about whether they should be compassionate? Remind the students that it isn't always easy to be compassionate, particularly toward certain people. Ask them to write in their journal about specific compassionate things they will do for a difficult person they know. Give them a few minutes to do this.

(Write one situation each on paper ahead of time.)
Pass out situation cards to different students and ask them to read aloud and tell what they would do in each situation.

1. Once I helped a friend by......
2. When someone is sick, I can.....
3. Once someone showed compassion for me by.....
4. You are playing soccer in the street and you see a blind man with a cane suddenly fall, so you......
5. There is a new student in your class who sits alone at recess.....
6. Someone you don't know is being made fun of and you witness this, so you....

Activity D–Read story about Orca whales

Did you know that an Orca whale can weigh as much as 18,000 pounds? They can grow up to 35 feet long, live to be 75 years old, and travel at speeds of 30 mph in the ocean. Orca whales are very smart and easy to train. They love to be petted and like to please their trainers.

40

Sometimes they even make up their own tricks and teach them to their trainers. One important way that Orca whales prove how smart they are is the way they show compassion for other Orcas. When one Orca whale calls for help, members of their family can tell they are in trouble and will quickly come to help. Even if it means risking their own life, Orcas will help any other Orca that is in trouble. When a whale becomes sick and has trouble breathing, one or two other whales will lift it to the surface so that it won't drown. Sometimes whales get beached or stuck where the water is too shallow, trying to help another whale. Scientists believe that these whales have strong social ties because of the way they communicate and care for each other. Although they are strong and fierce mammals, Orca whales seem to care enough to help their friends when they have a problem.

Activity E–Make "Compassion Cards"

Pass out a piece of paper to each student. Using crayons or markers, have each student make a "Compassion Card" for someone who may need it. Cards should say, "I'm thinking of you" or "Have a great day!" (They can also just say thanks or I love you!) Tell them to give these to people whom they admire or are grateful to have in their life.

Activity F–Show the "Love Eggs-periment"

Show the students an egg and give it a name. Draw a sad face on it. Tell the class that this egg (person) is not feeling good about them self. They don't do well in school. They don't have many friends. Their clothes are old and they don't get much attention at home. Carefully place an egg in the glass of water and observe how it sinks to the bottom. Tell the students that the egg represents someone who is not receiving love or acceptance from those around them. Sinking to the bottom represents how someone who is ridiculed or made fun of would feel. They might feel low, sad, depressed, or unappreciated.

Remove the egg from the water and set it aside. One tablespoon at a time, add the salt to the water. As you stir in each spoonful, explain that the salt represents different ways to make this person feel loved and accepted. Use examples that are relevant to your student's life such as, offering to eat lunch with the student at school, bringing cookies to them, helping them with their homework, asking them if they want to come over to their house sometime, etc. After you have added all of the salt, stir the water. Replace the egg to show how it is now supported with "Love" and "Held up" by the encouragement and acceptance. It should float. Discuss how being loved feels like you're floating. Draw a happy face on the other side of the egg!

Activity G–Showing Compassion for classmates

Have each student tear out a blank page of their journal and write their name on it. Tell them to fold the paper in half and that you will be collecting them. After you collect the papers, mix them up and pass out to the students so that they don't get their own name. Tell them that for the month, their duty will be to show compassion toward the person on their paper. Tell them not to let the person they have received know you have their name. Giving service is always better anonymously.

Activity H–Read Poem

He drew a circle that shut me out
Heretic rebel a thing to flout
But love and I had the wit to win
We drew a circle that took him in.

Ask the students what this poem means to them. Can they think of examples from their own lives that seem to fit with this poem? Ask them if there is anyone who can benefit from being drawn into their circle? (Heretic means one who maintains religious beliefs at variance, and Flout means to treat with disdain or contempt)

Display the following quotes and have the students write them in their journals.

1. "To ease another's heartache is to forget one's own". Abraham Lincoln
2. "Be the change you want to see in the world". Mahatma Ghandi
3. "If you can't feed a hundred people, then just feed one". Mother Teresa

Summarize the lesson by telling the students that reaching out to others makes life meaningful. What is really great about this is that the more you give, the more you will receive. You will be happier in life, and your self-esteem will be better.

Collect all journals and Spotlight papers from the students. You can hand back each of the Spotlight papers after you have checked to make sure all of the comments are positive.

SELF-DISCIPLINE

Objectives
-Spotlight
-Discuss the meaning of Self-Discipline
-Pose scenarios of Self-Discipline
-Read story about Apolo Ohno and Tony Hawk
-Show "Goalies" object lesson
-Discuss goal setting and write personal goals

Materials
-A journal for every student
-Construction paper for 3-4 Spotlights
-A goal setting sheet for each student
-A handful of pennies or other coins

Before you start the lesson, ask the students about showing compassion for another student from the last lesson. They were to do this for the student whose name appeared on the piece of paper they received during last months lesson and try to keep their compassion for this person as anonymous as possible.

Activity A–Spotlight

Tell the students that you are going to start the lesson by doing Spotlight. Pick one journal without letting the students see which one you pick. Read the answers to the Spotlight questions in that journal and see if someone can guess whose answers you've read. You can either have the students stand and then sit when an answer is not theirs, leaving the last person standing, or you can read the answers and at the end choose a student to guess. After the person is guessed, ask them to come to the front of the class. Ask them more questions about themselves such as pets, siblings, hobbies, etc. Next, ask members of the class to say 5 nice things about this person being Spotlighted. While they are doing this write the name of the student being Spotlighted in the center of a piece of construction paper. Pass around the sheet and let all students write something positive about that person all over the page. When the paper is done being passed around to each student, you will collect it and give it to the student at the end of the lesson.

Make sure all of the comments are positive before handing back to the student. Also, write the word "Done" on the front of each journal of those you have Spotlighted so you don't repeat. You will Spotlight about 3-4 students during each lesson depending on how many are in the class.

Pass out the remaining journals.

Activity B–Discuss the meaning of Self-Discipline

Tell the students that today you are going to talk about self-discipline. Ask them if they know the definition of the word. Write on the board, **self-discipline is the ability to be in control of your actions so you can make good choices.** Have them write this definition in their journals. Tell them that self-discipline is required to accomplish any task. Completing projects on time or just being consistent with their daily routine requires self-discipline. Point to self-discipline on the board and ask a student to identify how many "I"s and "U"s there are in the word. After they see there are only "I"s and no "U"s, tell them that having self discipline involves "I" not "U". It is something "I" should choose to do, and not expect "U" to do for me. Have the students write three statements in their journals that begin with "I". For example, "I will take care of my things" or "I will listen to my teacher". Encourage students to share their statements with the class.

Talk about how being self-disciplined means doing what is needed, even if you don't feel like it at the time. Write on the board these three sentences, and have the students fill in the blanks. "_____ needed to be done. Instead I wanted to _____. But I choose to be self-disciplined and _____ happened." Steer the students toward the topics of homework and chores to make this more interesting.

Activity C–Pose scenarios of Self-Discipline

Pose the following scenarios to the class. Ask students to give a "thumbs up" or "thumbs down" to show whether they have enough self-discipline to accomplish the named task.

1. Run a mile without stopping.
2. Choose to eat carrot sticks instead of potato chips at lunch.
3. Turn off the computer game before it is over and go to bed.
4. Choose not to hit their sibling back after he or she hits them first.
5. Finish a project and turn it in before it is due.

Ask, "Why is it so hard to have self-discipline? How could you be more successful if you showed more self-discipline in your life?"

Activity D–Read stories about Apolo Ohno and Tony Hawk

Apolo Anton Ohno was born May 22, 1982. His father was Japanese and his mother was Caucasian. They divorced when he was an infant. He was raised by his father. In his early years, swimming was his passion. When he was 12, he won the Washington State Championship for his age group in the Breast Stroke. But he now preferred inline speed skating over swimming. At age 13, Ohno decided to become a short-track skater. He trained at the Lake Placid Olympic Training Center in 1996. His teammates nicknamed him "Chunky", which motivated him to train harder. During the 1997 US Senior Championships, he won a Gold Medal in the 1500 meter event. He competed in 3 Olympic Games. He is the most decorated American Winter Olympic athlete as of the 2010 Winter Olympics. In preparation for the 2010 Winter Games, Ohno lost over 20 pounds of weight with an intense training program. In response to his training regimen, Ohno said, "Come these Games, there is no one who is going to be fitter than me. There's just no way. Whether I can put it together on the ice or not and feel good, that's a different story. But I know from a physical training standpoint, nobody's even close. I've never prepared like this in my life for anything. I want to leave nothing on the table".

Tony Hawk got his first skateboard when he was 9 years old. Five years later, when was 14, he turned pro. When he was 17, his high school "Careers" teacher scolded him in front of the entire class for jumping ahead in his workbook. He told him that he would never make it in the work place if he didn't follow directions explicitly. He said he would never make a living as a skateboarder. Even during those dark years, he never stopped riding his skateboard and never stopped progressing as a skater. There were many times when he was frustrated because he couldn't land a maneuver. But he realized that the only way to master something is to keep at it. Despite the bloody knees, the twisted ankles, and the mocking crowds, he set his goal to succeed. He kept on going regardless of what people said. Tony hopes to pass on the lesson to young people to find the thing that you love, and work hard to succeed at it.

These two professionals show us that with hard work and self-discipline you can achieve the desires and dreams of your heart.

Activity E–"Goalies" object lesson

Explain to the students that they should all have goals in their lives. Goals can be small or big, short term or long term. To accomplish any goal, a person needs self-discipline. Choose one student from the class to come up to the front of the class. Put some coins in your hand. Show the student the coins and tell them that these are special coins called "Goalies". Stand a few feet away from the student and ask them if they can catch the "Goalies" when you toss them. Then toss the handful of coins to them. Naturally they will go all over the place, and the student will probably only catch 1 or 2. Now try it again, except now toss just one coin at a time to the student. They should be able to catch them. Explain that the reason these coins are called "Goalies" is that they are like goals. When we try to work on too many goals at the same time, it can be difficult, and most of the goals won't be accomplished. When we catch one at a time, we have more success. Ask the students to share some of their goals and how they used self-discipline to accomplish them.

Activity F–Discuss Goal setting and write personal goals

Tell the students that they should all have short term and long term goals. They are more likely to achieve personal accomplishments if they have been written down. Explain the process of setting goals. Have them write in their journals the following:

1. Define the goal.
2. Outline the steps needed to achieve it.
3. Consider possible blocks and ways of dealing with them.
4. Set deadlines.

Pass out a "Goal Setting" handout to each student. Have them write down a specific goal and the necessary steps to achieve it. Give them a few minutes to do this and ask for volunteers to share their goals. Remind the students that self-discipline is very important when trying to achieve their goals. Every step in their plan is critical, after all, "A journey of a thousand miles begins with just one step."

Summarize the lesson by telling the students that accomplishing anything takes effort. Some things might take more effort than others. When you accomplish something hard by using self-discipline you will have better self-esteem.

Collect all journals and Spotlight papers from the students. You can hand back each of the Spotlight papers after you have checked to make sure all of the comments are positive.

Name_____

GOAL SETTING

Set Reachable Goals.
Write out steps for reaching that goal.
Keep going until you reach your goal.
Give yourself a reasonable time limit.
Evaluate – Check your progress.
Compliment yourself.

My Goal is _____

1		
2		
3		
4		

H O N E S T Y

Objectives
-Spotlight
-Discuss the meaning of honesty
-Play Two Truths and a Lie
-Read story about Goose
-The "All Tied Up" object lesson
-Scenarios on Honesty

Materials
-A journal for every student
-Construction paper for 3-4 Spotlights
-A ball of Yarn

Activity A–Spotlight

Tell the students that you are going to start the lesson by doing Spotlight. Pick one journal without letting the students see which one you pick. Read the answers to the Spotlight questions in that journal and see if someone can guess whose answers you've read. You can either have the students stand and then sit when an answer is not theirs, leaving the last person standing, or you can read the answers and at the end choose a student to guess. After the person is guessed, ask them to come to the front of the class. Ask them more questions about themselves such as pets, siblings, hobbies, etc. Next, ask members of the class to say 5 nice things about this person being Spotlighted. While they are doing this write the name of the student being Spotlighted in the center of a piece of construction paper. Pass around the sheet and let all students write something positive about that person all over the page. When the paper is done being passed around to each student, you will collect it and give it to the student at the end of the lesson.

Make sure all of the comments are positive before handing back to the student. Also, write the word "Done" on the front of each journal of those you have Spotlighted so you don't repeat. You will Spotlight about 3-4 students during each lesson depending on how many are in the class.

Pass out the remaining journals.

Activity B–Discuss the meaning of Honesty

Ask the students if they know what honesty means. Have them write in their journals the definition as you write it on the chalkboard. **Honesty is watching what you say and do so others will trust you.** Honesty is necessary if you are to learn to trust and be trusted. It requires an accurate reporting of the facts and telling others what they need to hear. Ask the students "What Honesty means to them". Ask them if they are always honest. Ask if there is a time when you think it is okay not to be honest. Ask them if they want others to be honest with them, and why. Lead a discussion on each of these topics. And lastly, ask this important question. "What would you do if you were walking in your neighborhood and found a bag with $1000 in it?"

Activity C–Play Two Truths and a Lie

Ask the students to write down three sentences on a page in their journals and number each sentence. Two of these sentences should be something true about them, and one of the sentences should be a lie. Some of the statements could be about where they live, where they were born, their favorite book, etc. Instruct them to write their name on the top of their paper. Instruct the students to rip out this page and collect them from each student. Read them and see if the students can identify the one lie in each page.

Activity D–Read the story about Goose

Sometimes when you look up at the sky, you can see birds flying in the shape of a "V". It is the way geese travel when they are going south for the winter. A Canadian Goose can grow up to be 4 feet tall with wings that stretch out as far as 6 feet. The goose that lies in front cuts through the wind so flying can be easier for the rest of the geese. By following the lead goose, the rest of the flock can reach their destination faster and with fewer stops along the way. When the bird in front gets tired, it moves to the back of the flock and another bird takes it's place. Geese have to learn to trust each other. Those who lead have to go the right direction, and those who follow have to know they can depend on the actions of the goose that is leading. Honesty works a lot like a lead goose. When you are honest, it helps others trust you. When you are careful about what you say and do, everyone around you will learn to trust you and you will learn to trust them.

Activity E–The "All Tied Up" object lesson

Choose one student to come up to the front of the class. Whisper in their ear to give you a false answer to any of the questions that you ask. Have the student sit in a chair where the class can see them. Start out by asking them a simple question. For example, "I heard that you found $20 on the playground?" As the student answers you with a lie (in this case, the answer being Yes), wrap a long string of yarn around them once. Then ask them a follow up question based on the first reply, such as, "What did you buy with that money?" Continue to ask a line of questions to the student involving this same incident, while wrapping more yarn around the student each time he tells a lie. Eventually they will be tied to the chair, entangled in a web of yarn.

After the students observe them in this tangled mess, explain that you asked this student to make up answers to all of my questions. Then discuss some of the following ideas:

1. What can telling lies do to someone? Emphasize how one lie usually leads to another and how we can quickly become trapped.

2. Ask the students to tell about times when they have been caught in a lie.
3. Ask why it is important to always tell the truth.

Activity F–Scenarios on Honesty

Read the following scenarios and have students respond with correct answers for each.

1. Stephanie went to the grocery store with her mom. While she was at the store, she saw a candy bar that she really wanted. She didn't have any money. She put the candy bar in her pocket anyway. Was this honest? What should she do?
2. Jason wanted to go to the school football game with his friends. His mom said he couldn't go to the game but had to go to a church activity instead. Jason agreed, but when he left the house, he went to the football game instead. Was this honest? What should Jason do?
3. Megan was having a hard time in her math class at school. The final exam was coming quickly and she hadn't studied for it. Her best friend, Lisa, said that she could look at her answers during the test. Is Megan being honest? Is Lisa being honest? What should they do?
4. Amy told her best friend, Melissa, a personal secret. Melissa promised not to tell anyone. When Amy wasn't around, Melissa told Amy's secret to others. Was this honest? What should Melissa do?

Summarize the lesson by reminding the students that they should strive to be honest with themselves and everyone around them. And that when they do, this will raise their self-esteem.

Collect all journals and Spotlight papers from the students. You can hand back each of the Spotlight papers after you have checked to make sure all of the comments are positive.

GRATITUDE

Objectives
-Spotlight
-Discuss the meaning of Gratitude
-Make Gratitude List
-Gratitude Questions
-Pebble in the Shoe
-Happiness Test

Materials
-A journal for every student
-Construction paper for 3-4 Spotlights
-1 small pebble (rock) and a piece of candy

Activity A–Spotlight

Tell the students that you are going to start the lesson by doing Spotlight. Pick one journal without letting the students see which one you pick. Read the answers to the Spotlight questions in that journal and see if someone can guess whose answers you've read. You can either have the students stand and then sit when an answer is not theirs, leaving the last person standing, or you can read the answers and at the end choose a student to guess. After the person is guessed, ask them to come to the front of the class. Ask them more questions about themselves such as pets, siblings, hobbies, etc. Next, ask members of the class to say 5 nice things about this person being Spotlighted. While they are doing this write the name of the student being Spotlighted in the center of a piece of construction paper. Pass around the sheet and let all students write something positive about that person all over the page. When the paper is done being passed around to each student, you will collect it and give it to the student at the end of the lesson.

Make sure all of the comments are positive before handing back to the student. Also. write the word "Done" on the front of each journal of those you have Spotlighted so you don't repeat. You will Spotlight about 3-4 students during each lesson depending on how many are in the class.

Pass out all journals

Activity B–Discuss the meaning of Gratitude

Tell the students that today you are going to be talking about Gratitude. Write the word on the board and have them write the definition in their journals. **Gratitude is a feeling or attitude in acknowledgement of a benefit one has received.** Discuss why saying thank you is a very important action. When thanks is given, both parties are affected in a positive way. When you say thank you to someone who has shown you kindness, it motivates that person to want to do more good deeds for that individual as well as others. Recognizing the blessings in your life and acting upon them regularly increases your awareness and appreciation. Your gratitude improves the quality of life because it can only result in positive emotions. Learning to appreciate what you have also makes life more valuable and meaningful.

Activity C—Make a Gratitude List

Have the students write in their journals 10 things that they are grateful for and why. An example of something they might be grateful for could be their teacher, because of all the time that is spent in preparation for their instruction. Have a few students share some of their answers.

Activity D—Gratitude Questions

Ask the students why they are grateful for the following.

1. Our Country
2. Our Body
3. Our Home
4. Scientific Discoveries
5. The Earth
6. Music
7. Family
8. School

Activity E—Pebble in the shoe

Pick a student to come to the front of the room. Have them take off one shoe and put a small pebble inside of their shoe. Have the student then put their shoe back on. Then give them a piece of candy to eat immediately. With the pebble in their shoe, and candy in their mouth, have them walk around the room. When they are finished, ask them which experience they noticed more. Would the candy have been more enjoyable to eat without the pebble as a distraction? Explain that when we are ungrateful and complain, it is like we have a pebble in our shoe. We don't fully experience all our blessings, and we don't notice them as easily.

Activity F—Happiness Test

Tell the students if they ever complain about not having a swimming pool, latest style clothes, or not being able to go on an elaborate vacation, that you are going to give them the following test.

1. Over 700 million people in the world, according to the United Nations, are starving. Do you have plenty of different kinds of food to eat?
2. Over 500 million people in the world do not have permanent weather proof shelter to live in. Do you have a home to live in?

3. Only one out of 7,000 people in the world has a TV to watch. How many TV's do you have in your home?

4. Over 800 million people in the world have only one set of clothes to wear. Many more than that have no shoes or coat. Do you have enough different kinds of clothes to wear?

5. Over 700 million people in the world die every year because they do not have access to a doctor or medicine. When you get sick, is there a doctor and medicine available to help you get well?

6. Only 1 out of every 750 children in the world has the chance to learn to read and write. How many books do you have in your house?

7. Over 960 million people in the world have no restaurants of any kinds available to them. How many restaurants can you name that you have been to in the last year?

To summarize the lesson, ask the class if someone can think of a negative situation that has happened to them. Use this example and ask the class to give you 10 positive things that they can name about this situation. This will teach the students that in any negative situation, there are always positive things that come out of it. Tell the class that by being aware of what they are grateful for, they have all raised their self-esteem.

Collect all journals and Spotlight papers from the students. You can hand back each of the Spotlight papers after you have checked to make sure all of the comments are positive

FORGIVENESS

Objectives
-Finish Spotlights
-Discuss the meaning of Forgiveness
-Object lesson on Forgiveness
-Final review of Project Self Esteem

Materials
-A journal for every student
-Enough construction paper to finish Spotlights
-1 clear glass, vinegar, bleach, water, food coloring
-Prizes

Activity A–Spotlight

Tell the students that you are going to start the lesson by doing Spotlight. Pick one journal without letting the students see which one you pick. Read the answers to the Spotlight questions in that journal and see if someone can guess whose answers you've read. You can either have the students stand and then sit when an answer is not theirs, leaving the last person standing, or you can read the answers and at the end choose a student to guess. After the person is guessed, ask them to come to the front of the class. Ask them more questions about themselves such as pets, siblings, hobbies, etc. Next, ask members of the class to say 5 nice things about this person being Spotlighted. While they are doing this write the name of the student being Spotlighted in the center of a piece of construction paper. Pass around the sheet and let all students write something positive about that person all over the page. When the paper is done being passed around to each student, you will collect it and give it to the student at the end of the lesson. **Finish all Spotlights since this is the last lesson.**

Pass out the remaining journals.

Activity B–Discuss the meaning of Forgiveness

Tell the class that today you are going to discuss the meaning of Forgiveness. Have them open their journals and write the following definition. **Forgiveness is deciding that someone who has wronged you doesn't have to pay.** Tell them that there are 4 basic steps to have forgiveness.

1. Be Sympathetic and listen with an open heart.
2. Bring both people together to see the problem from both sides.
3. Talk to the person who has hurt you because usually problems can be solved here with it being a simple misunderstanding.
4. Be patient and let each person talk without interruption.

The students must realize that forgiving someone does not take the hurt away, it just starts the healing process. Also, discuss why it is a good thing to show forgiveness. Have the students take out a piece of paper from their journals. Ask them to write about a time when someone wronged them. Ask them not to put their name on it. Collect all papers and choose several to read aloud and have the students brainstorm ways they can show forgiveness in each situation. Then ask the students what it would be like if no one in the world showed forgiveness.

Activity C–Object lesson on Forgiveness

Show the class a clear glass. Pour the mixture of water and vinegar into the glass. Tell the class that the cup represents a boy named Warren. Tell the class that you are going to tell them a story about Warren. Warren was a young boy who always seemed to get into trouble. One day he was walking to school and throwing rocks along the way when he accidentally broke a house window. He ran to school and never told anyone about it. (Add a drop of food coloring to the glass). Continue the story adding several more instances of Warren getting into trouble and lying about it, such as stealing money or cheating on a test, etc. As you relate the story, add a drop of food coloring to Warren's glass each time he does something wrong. Point out that the first time Warren did something wrong, the color didn't affect too much of the water. But each additional time he did something wrong, "He" became darker and cloudier. The stain had finally permeated his entire being and filled him with guilt. Eventually Warren felt miserable. His friends didn't want to be around him because he was always getting into trouble, and they couldn't trust him. He decided to talk with the Principal and his parents and he wanted to change his ways. First he went to the neighbor and apologized for the broken window and offered to pay for the damages. Then he went and confessed his other wrong doings. As you tell this part of the story with examples of how Warren has asked for forgiveness, add a drop of bleach with each example. Eventually the glass will become clear again. Ask the class how they think Warren feels about himself now that he has asked for forgiveness. Ask them if they know the steps they need to go through to make amends for an act of dishonesty.

1. Recognize they have done something wrong.
2. Apologize to the person they have offended.
3. Repair the relationship.
4. Resolve not to do it again.

Summarize the lesson by telling the students that their self esteem will be better if they will ask for forgiveness when they have wronged another. Have them journal the following quote. "Holding on to anger is like grasping a hot coal with the intent of throwing it at someone else; you are the one getting burned."

Jautama Budda

Activity D–Final review of Project Self-Esteem

Before the lesson, read through the previous lessons from this past year and write down some questions to ask the class about the subjects you have taught.

Explain that they have used their journals to take notes on the lessons you have taught. They may use their notes to answer your questions. To make it more fun, bring prizes for the students to give when they answer your questions correctly. Prizes could be pencils, stickers, snacks, etc.

End the lesson by telling the students that you have enjoyed helping them learn what good self-esteem means. Tell them that they are the only ones that have the greatest opportunity to compliment themselves. This means that they are the ones that create their own Self-Esteem. No one can ultimately make them believe that they are not good enough. They always have the choice to do better and act better. In turn, they will feel good about themselves.

Pass out the remaining Spotlight papers making sure that all comments are positive.

(The journals are for the students to keep.)

RESPECT

Objectives
-Introduce Spotlight
-Discuss the meaning of Respect
-Role Play on Respect
-Drawing activity on Respect
-Respect Chart on chalkboard

Materials
-A journal for every student
-Construction paper for 3-4 Spotlights

Activity A–Introduction of facilitator, Project Self-Esteem and Spotlight

Tell the students your name and a little bit about yourself. Tell them that you are here to teach Project Self-Esteem. Self-esteem is how you feel about yourself. If you feel good about yourself, you will be happy and will treat others well. Explain that your goal is to teach them to have good self-esteem through these lessons. Tell them that each one of them is special and this year you are going to find out why.

Pass out a journal to each student and ask them to write their name on the front cover. Tell the students that these journals are for them to take notes in during each of your lessons. Explain that when they take notes, they will better remember what you have taught. They will have their notes to refer to at the last lesson where you will have a review of the entire year. Now have the students open to the first page and write the date and number the lines 1 to 10. Ask the 10 following questions:

1. What is your favorite color?
2. What is your favorite food?
3. What is your favorite restaurant?
4. What is your favorite movie or T.V. show?
5. What is your favorite sport?
6. What is your favorite thing to do in your free time?
7. What is a talent that you have?
8. Where is a place that you would like to visit?
9. What would you like to be when you grow up?
10. Who is a person you admire? (dead or alive)

When you are done asking the questions, tell the students you are going to play a game called Spotlight with them at the end of the lesson. Have them turn to the next page in their journals and tell them they should be taking notes throughout the lesson.

Activity B–Discuss the meaning of Respect

Tell the students that today you are going to discuss the meaning of Respect. Write the word on the board and ask if anyone knows the definition. After answers are given, write the definition on the board and tell the students to write it in their journals. **Respect is showing others they are important by what you say or do.** People who understand and use respect will be better members of society, better friends, and better leaders. There are many ways to show respect. You show it by how you treat other people and yourself. You have to respect yourself before you can respect others. You show it by caring about other living things like animals, trees, air, and water. You show it by following rules and laws. You show it by paying attention to people's beliefs and customs.

Activity C–Role play Respect

Select two students to come to the front of the class. Tell them that you are going to give them a scenario to act out showing ways to use or not to use respect. After the first example, choose new pairs of students each time.

Scenario 1: Child is talking and not paying attention while the teacher is speaking.
Scenario 2: Child is polite and says, "No thank you Mr. Green" when offered something they don't want.
Scenario 3: Children push themselves in front of an older lady at the checkout stand in the grocery store.
Scenario 4: Child holds their mother's chair as they sit down to eat and then says, "Thanks for the nice dinner mom."
Scenario 5: Child gets upset after losing in a kickball game and kicks the ball far away after the teacher asks them to pick it up.
Scenario 6: Child keeps interrupting his mother while she is trying to talk to a friend on the phone.

Ask the class if they could tell when respect was shown. Lead a discussion on how the students should show respect for others around them and how it will benefit them as well as the person they are respecting.

Activity D–Drawing activity on Respect

Have the students draw in their journals a picture of a person they respect such as a family member, sports hero, teacher, or friend and write about why they respect them.

After they are done writing about the person they respect, ask if a few of them would like to share their comments with the class.

Next, have the students think about the most important item they own. Ask them to think about leaving that item with someone to take care of it. What if that person did not treat that item with respect? What if the item came back broken or not at all? Discuss what might happen. Then have them tell you about how they would take care of someone else's item if they were given the opportunity. Have one person lend an item that they have to someone else in the class just for a day and see if they can treat the item with respect. (An example might be a pencil, book, or other personal item.)

Activity E–Make a Respect Chart on chalkboard

Make a chart on the chalkboard with the heading saying **RESPECT CHART.** Under this heading, write on the left side of the board **WHO/WHAT**, and on the right side write **HOW.**

RESPECT CHART

WHO/WHAT   **HOW**

This chart helps the students PLAN to be respectful. Using the left-hand column, ask the students to list categories of people and things that deserve respect. As you list them one at a time, discuss how respect for that person or thing can be given effectively.

Activity F–Spotlight

Collect all of the journals. Pick one journal without letting the students see which one you pick. Read the answers to the Spotlight questions in that journal and see if someone can guess whose answers you've read. You can either have the students stand and then sit when an answer is not theirs, leaving the last student standing, or you can read the answers and at the end choose a student to guess. After the person is guessed, ask them to come to the front of the class. Ask them more questions about themselves such as pets, siblings, hobbies, etc. Next, ask members of the class to say 5 nice things about this person being Spotlighted. While they are doing this, write the name of the student being Spotlighted in the center of a piece of construction paper. Pass around the sheet and let all of the students write something positive about that person all over the page. When the paper is done being passed around to each student, you will collect it and give it to the student.

Make sure all of the comments are positive before handing back to the student. Also, write the word "Done" on the front of each journal of those you have Spotlighted so you don't repeat. You will Spotlight about 3-4 students during each lesson depending on how many are in the class.

Tell the class that these Spotlight papers are for them to keep in a safe place. If they are having a bad day and not feeling good about themselves, then they can get out this paper and see the positive comments that were made about them. This should raise their self-esteem!

UNIQUENESS

Objectives
-Spotlight
-Discuss the meaning of Uniqueness
-Take "The Real Me" quiz
-Play the "Special Me" Game
-Art project on Uniqueness

Materials
-A journal for every student
-Construction paper for 3-4 Spotlights
-A copy of "The Real Me" quiz for every student
-A piece of paper for every student

Activity A–Spotlight

Tell the students that you are going to start the lesson by doing Spotlight. Pick one journal without letting the students see which one you pick. Read the answers to the Spotlight questions in that journal and see if someone can guess whose answers you've read. You can either have the students stand and then sit when an answer is not theirs, leaving the last person standing, or you can read the answers and at the end, choose a student to guess. After the person is guessed, ask them to come to the front of the class. Ask them more questions about themselves such as pets, siblings, hobbies, etc. Next, ask members of the class to say 5 nice things about this person being Spotlighted. While they are doing this, write the name of the student being Spotlighted in the center of a piece of construction paper. Pass around the sheet and let all students write something positive about that person all over the page. When the paper is done being passed around to each student, you will collect it and give it to the student at the end of the lesson.

Make sure all of the comments are positive before handing back to the student. Also, write the word "Done" on the front of each journal of those you have Spotlighted so you don't repeat. You will Spotlight about 3-4 students during each lesson depending on how many are in the class.

Pass out all of the journals.

Activity B–Discuss the meaning of Uniqueness

Tell the students that today you are going to talk about being unique. Ask if anyone knows the definition of Uniqueness. After choosing a few responses, write the definition on the board and have the students write it in their journals. **Uniqueness is learning more about others so you can know more about yourself.** As a class, discuss the importance of being an individual. One uses their individual talents to make a difference in the world. Discuss what it would be like if we all looked the same, acted the same, and had the same talents in the world. BORING!!! Have the students write in their journals, "I am different because I.........." Some of them might like to share their responses.

Activity C–Take "The Real Me" quiz

Pass out to each student "The Real Me" quiz. Tell them that you will give them a few minutes to complete the quiz. After they are done, ask for volunteers to share some of their answers. This activity will show that students might have different responses to situations and that is what makes them unique.

Activity D–Play the "Special Me" Game

Have each student tear out a piece of paper from their journals. Have them write their name on one side. Collect all of the papers and then pass them out so no one gets their own name. Tell them to write a compliment about that person such as, "beautiful hair, best dressed, very athletic, etc." Have them think of unique things to say about that person. Collect the papers and put them into a hat or jar. Take out each slip of paper and read the compliment and have the class guess who the student is being described.

Activity E–Art project on Uniqueness

Pass out a piece of paper to each student. Talk about how their fingerprints are unique and there will never be another one like them. Have the students trace one hand and cut it out. On each of the five fingers have the students list one thing on each finger that makes them unique. They should end up with five unique things about themselves. Display the hands somewhere in the room so the students can see them for the month to remind them of the lesson.

Write on the board the following quote and have the students write it in their journals.

"Always be a first-rate version of yourself, instead of a second-rate version of somebody else." – Judy Garland

End the lesson by telling the students that each one of them is unique and that they should appreciate themselves and others for being unique. When they do this they will have better self-esteem.

Collect all of the journals and Spotlight papers from the students and pass out each of the Spotlight papers after you have checked to make sure all of the comments are positive.

Name_____

THE REAL ME

I think I am.....   (Put a Check mark by the best answer)

_____Quiet as a mouse
or
_____Noisy as a firecracker
_____A little of both

_____Fast as a cheetah
or
_____Slow as a turtle
_____A little of both

_____Super neat
or
_____Super messy
_____A little of both

_____An indoor kid
or
_____An outdoor kid
_____A little of both

_____A talker
or
_____A listener
_____A little of both

J O Y

Objectives
-Spotlight
-Play Pictionary and discuss the meaning of Joy
-Drawing activity on Joy
-Discuss Joy scenarios using Sad and Happy Faces
-Make Joy Lists

Materials
-A journal for every student
-3-4 pieces of construction paper for Spotlights
-Slips of paper with the words: smile, laugh, party, and happy
-Cut out copies of Sad and Happy Face

Activity A–Spotlight

Tell the students that you are also going to start the lesson by doing Spotlight. Pick one journal without letting the students see which one you pick. Read the answers to the Spotlight questions in that journal and see if someone can guess whose answers you've read. You can either have the students stand and then sit when an answer is not theirs, leaving the last person standing, or you can read the answers and at the end, choose a student to guess. After the person is guessed, ask them to come to the front of the class. Ask them more questions about themselves such as pets, siblings, hobbies, etc. Next, ask members of the class to say 5 nice things about this person being Spotlighted. While they are doing this, write the name of the student being Spotlighted in the center of a piece of construction paper. Pass around the sheet and let all students write something positive about that person all over the page. When the paper is done being passed around to each student, you will collect it and give it to the student at the end of the lesson.

Make sure all of the comments are positive before handing back to the student. Also, write the word "Done" on the front of each journal of those you have Spotlighted so you don't repeat. You will Spotlight about 3-4 students during each lesson depending on how many are in the class.

Pass out all of the journals.

Activity B–Play Pictionary and discuss the meaning of Joy

Tell the students that you are going to start the lesson by playing Pictionary. Tell them that you are going to have them guess your topic today with the game of Pictionary. Let one student at a time come to the chalkboard to draw a picture. The rest of the class will guess what they are drawing. Use word strips that say smile, laugh, party, and happy. Once the words have all been guessed, ask the students what all of the words have in common. Their guesses should lead you to the word JOY. Have them write the definition of joy in their journals. **Joy is finding a way to be happy, even when things don't go your way.** Tell them that joy is more than being happy. It's an attitude that one can share with others around them. Joy is not in things; it is in us.

Activity C–Drawing Joy

Tell the students to draw in their journals a picture of a smiley face while looking at the ceiling. When they are done, have them look at the pictures and discuss if they came out the way they had envisioned. Now have them draw the same picture, but let them look at their paper this time. Discuss the differences between the two pictures. The one that the students focused on has the desired outcome. Joy is the same way. When we focus on being happy, even when something isn't going our way, we will have a pleasant outcome: JOY!!

Activity D–Discuss Joy scenarios using Sad and Happy Faces

Have a student come to the front of the class. Show the smiling and frowning faces to the class. Give them to the student and tell them that you are going to read some situations and you want them to decide how they would react. Read the following scenarios; missed the bus, got an "A" on a test, got to be first in line, forgot your lunch money, little sister took your candy, and won a prize from a raffle. Have them hold up the face that would show how they would feel after each situation. Discuss how it is easy to respond with joy to the good things. Then brainstorm how they could respond with joy to the bad scenarios.

Activity E–Make Joy lists

Have the students write in their journals the letters J O Y. Then make a list of words that begin with these letters. Once they have made a list of at least ten words for each letter, have them circle the words that make them feel Joy. Then have them list the Top 10 things that make them happy. Have a few students share their lists.

Summarize the lesson by telling the students that having joy is an important part of life. No matter what is happening around you, there is always the choice to be happy. Joy is contagious. If we are happy then others around us will share our feelings. When we are happy, we want to do more for others. It always feels good to serve. We will have better self-esteem.

Collect all journals and Spotlight papers from the students. Pass out each of the Spotlight papers after you have checked to make sure all of the comments are positive.

Copy and cut out faces for student to use in activity.

DETERMINATION

Objectives
-Spotlight
-Discuss the meaning of Determination
-Read the story of "The Tortoise and the Hare"
-Discuss goals and make New Year's resolutions
-Object lesson "Knockout"

Materials
-A journal for every student
-3-4 pieces of construction paper for Spotlights
-Slips of paper with the definition of the word Determination
-Story of "The Tortoise and the Hare"
-Empty shoeboxes and post-it notes

Activity A–Spotlight

Tell the students that you are going to start the lesson by doing Spotlight. Pick one journal without letting the students see which one you pick. Read the answers to the Spotlight questions in that journal and see if someone can guess whose answers you've read. You can either have the students stand and then sit when an answer is not theirs, leaving the last person standing, or you can read the answers and at the end, choose a student to guess. After the person is guessed, ask them to come to the front of the class. Ask them more questions about themselves such as pets, siblings, hobbies, etc. Next, ask members of the class to say 5 nice things about this person being Spotlighted. While they are doing this, write the name of the student being Spotlighted in the center of a piece of construction paper. Pass around the sheet and let all students write something positive about that person all over the page. When the paper is done being passed around to each student, you will collect it and give it to the student at the end of the lesson. Do this for 3-4 students.

Make sure all of the comments are positive before handing back to the student. Also, write the word "Done" on the front of each journal of those you have Spotlighted so you don't repeat. You will Spotlight about 3-4 students during each lesson depending on how many are in the class.

Pass out all of the journals.

Activity B–Discuss the meaning of Determination

Tell the students that today you are going to discuss the meaning of Determination. Tell the class that you have the definition of determination and that you have split it into 9 parts. Choose 9 students to come up to the front of the class and put the definition in the correct order. Have the class write the definition in their journals once it is correct. **Determination is deciding it's worth it to finish what you've started.** Ask the students if they have ever started something but didn't finish it. This could be not finishing reading a book, starting piano lessons but dropping out, etc. Discuss how they felt when they first started, (excitement and eagerness). Then discuss what it was that made them quit. Write the word Determination on the board. Have the students think of synonyms of the word such as courage, bravery, will power, etc. After a few minutes, allow the students time to share some of their answers. Add their answers underneath the word "Determination" on the board.

Activity C–Read the story of "The Tortoise and the Hare"

Read the following story of "The Tortoise and the Hare" and discuss how we win many of life's rewards by learning how to hang in there and work until the very end.

A hare once made fun of a tortoise. "What a slow way you have!" he said. "How you creep along!"

"Do I?" said the tortoise. "Try a race with me and I'll beat you."

"What a boaster you are," said the hare. "But come! I will race with you. Whom shall we ask to mark off the finish line and see that the race is fair?"

"Let's ask the fox," said the tortoise.

The fox was very wise and fair. He showed them where they were to start, and how far they were to run.

The tortoise lost no time. He started out at once and jogged straight on.

The hare leaped along swiftly for a few minutes until he had left the tortoise far behind. He knew he could reach the mark very quickly, so he lay down by the road under a shady tree and took a nap.

By and by he awoke and remembered the race. He sprang up and ran as fast as he could. But when he reached the mark the tortoise was already there!

"Slow and steady wins the race," said the fox.

AESOP

Have the students write in their journals the following:

"Yard by yard, it's so hard! Inch by inch, it's a cinch."
"Work like a stamp, it sticks to one thing until it gets there."
"Continuing to work hard is courage in a person, the coward gives up."

Tell the students that a person showing determination is not distracted easily by things or other people. Some people give up too easily and move from one thing to another without really giving it their best effort. (Ex. Sports) If you stick to something, you will reap the rewards. People will view you differently and admire you. There is personal satisfaction in achieving a goal. Take the Wright Brothers for example. They both were very determined and had a goal in mind that they could make a flying machine. Just think if the Wright Brothers had given up and decided not to try anymore. This is true with so many inventors. Have the students name some inventors and see where we would be without them. (Albert Einstein, Alexander Graham Bell, Bill Gates, etc.) Have the students write in their journals examples of how they showed determination in the past or when other people they know have shown determination. Ask them to think about some Olympians who have won medals and discuss what it might have taken for them to be a champion.

Activity D–Discuss goals and make New Year's resolutions

In January, people usually make New Year's resolutions. Discuss how keeping these resolutions take a lot of determination. Have the students decide on a New Year's resolution they can set for themselves. Have them write these in their journals. You can have a few students share with the class their ideas. Remind them to keep track of them and not get discouraged if they get off track. Tell them that they should always be working on goals in their lives. Some might be small and some might be big. They will have better self-esteem when they accomplish a goal.

Activity E–Object lesson "Knockout"

Choose a student to come to the front of the class. Ask them to share a goal that they would like to achieve. Write the goal on a post-it note and stick it to the wall. Next, discuss the things that would prevent them from accomplishing that goal. Write these obstacles on a few post-it notes and stick them on various boxes. Let the student stack the boxes to form a barrier between them and the goal that is on the wall. Now, discuss the student's special skills that will help them overcome their doubts or fears in accomplishing their goal. These can be things like creativity, positive thinking, quick learner, etc. As you talk, write these qualities on a post-it note and put it on the student's shirt. Talk about the fact that by having these special skills, the student can accomplish almost anything they set their mind to do. Tell them to face the barricade of boxes and with all their strength, break through. This activity can really give the student a sense of what it feels like to take action in accomplishing their goals.

Summarize the lesson by telling the students that with hard work and determination they can accomplish anything. Even if they fail at something they will learn from it and if they keep trying they will eventually achieve even hard things. Their self-esteem will improve along the way.

Collect all journals and Spotlight papers from the students. Pass out each of the Spotlight papers after you have checked to make sure all of the comments are positive.

KINDNESS

Objectives
-Spotlight
-Discuss the meaning of Kindness
-Introduce "Kids Catching Kids" Jar
-Make cards to show kindness
-A "Spoonful of Sugar" object lesson
-Read the story, "The Lost Skates"

Materials
-A journal for every student
-3-4 pieces of construction paper for Spotlight
-A jar labeled "Kids Catching Kids" with 3X5 cards inside
-1 piece of paper for each student
-A clear glass or bowl, a pepper shaker, 1 teaspoon of sugar, and a bar of soap

Activity A–Spotlight

Tell the students that you are going to start the lesson by doing Spotlight. Pick one journal without letting the students see which one you pick. Read the answers to the Spotlight questions in that journal and see if someone can guess whose answers you've read. You can either have the students stand and then sit when an answer is not theirs, leaving the last person standing, or you can read the answers and at the end, choose a student to guess. After the person is guessed, ask them to come to the front of the class. Ask them more questions about themselves such as pets, siblings, hobbies, etc. Next, ask members of the class to say 5 nice things about this person being Spotlighted. While they are doing this, write the name of the student being Spotlighted in the center of a piece of construction paper. Pass around the sheet and let all students write something positive about that person all over the page. When the paper is done being passed around to each student, you will collect it and give it to the student at the end of the lesson.

Make sure all of the comments are positive before handing back to the student. Also, write the word "Done" on the front of each journal of those you have Spotlighted so you don't repeat. You will Spotlight about 3-4 students during each lesson depending on how many are in the class.

Pass out all of the journals

Activity B–Discuss the meaning of Kindness

Write the word Kindness on the board along with the definition. **Kindness is showing others they are valuable by how you treat them.** Have the students copy the definition in their journals. Discuss with the class how it makes them feel when someone is kind to them. Have a few students share examples or situations when someone showed kindness to them and discuss how it made them feel. Talk about the "Golden Rule" which is to do unto others what you would have done unto you. For example, if they want to have good friends they need to be a good friend.

Activity C—Introduce the "Kids Catching Kids" jar

Show the students the jar labeled "Kids Catching Kids" and tell them that when they catch anyone in their class showing kindness, they are to write it down on a card and put it in the jar. Tell them that at the next project self-esteem lesson, the cards will be read out loud. Discuss ways that they can show kindness to other people outside their normal circle of friends. Discuss how other people possibly do not have as much as they do, and think of ways they could help them. Discuss random acts of kindness. Ask them how it makes them feel when they are kind to someone.

Activity D—Make cards to show kindness

Pass out a piece of paper to each student. Give them a few minutes to make a card for someone. Tell them to write a kind message to someone they admire. Tell them that this small act of kindness will make someone else very happy. People enjoy receiving notes that show love or appreciation for them.

Activity E—"A Spoonful of Sugar" object lesson

Take out a clear glass or bowl and fill it with water. Sprinkle pepper liberally on the water. Tell the class that the pepper represents the people around them. This could be friends, family, teachers, etc. Discuss the fact that how we get along with those people is largely determined by how we treat and speak to them. Words can be very powerful tools, either for good or bad. It is important to learn positive and kind ways of speaking to our friends. Now talk about an example of someone who does not use kind words when speaking to others. Tell the students that the bar of soap represents negative, harsh language. Touch the soap to the center of the water. The soap will repel the pepper and will cause it to be dispersed to the sides of the bowl. Make the comparison that when we speak unkindly to others, they won't want to be around us, and will want to scatter. Take a teaspoon of sugar and pour it in the center of the water. Compare the sugar to the sweetness of kind and thoughtful words. Talk about how being loving toward other people usually causes them to be drawn to us, and makes them want to be our friends. They will see how the sugar attracts the pepper back from the sides of the bowl.

Activity F—Read the story "The Lost Skates"

Tell the class that you are going to read them a short story on Kindness.

One afternoon Jimmy was sitting on the front porch, thinking about his lost skates. He was thinking about them because down the street, a little boy was skating back and forth. Watching this boy had made Jimmy think about his own skates. The boy went slowly up and down the street. He seemed to be just learning how to skate. As Jimmy came close, he was surprised to see that the boy's skates looked quite new. "They are just like mine", Jimmy thought. Just then, the boy skated past him and Jimmy saw printed on the straps the word "Jimmy". "Why, those are my skates!" shouted Jimmy.

He stepped in front of the boy and stopped him. "Where did you get my skates?" he demanded. The little boy stared at him with round, frightened eyes. "They're not your skates", he said, "They're mine". "The trash man gave them to me". "I don't care who gave them to you", said Jimmy crossly, "They are mine". "What is your name?" asked Jimmy. "Stephen", said the little boy.

"Well! See my name is Jimmy, and it is written right here. I printed it myself, Jimmy. So they are mine", said Jimmy. The little boy looked worried. "The trash man gave them to me. He found them in the gutter when they had been thrown away". "They must have rolled down the walk when I took them off", said Jimmy. He recalled the day when he fell down and hurt his cheek. "Well, anyway, I didn't throw them away. And they are mine. Give them to me!" The little boy sat down and began to tug obediently at the straps. "I guess you're right", said the little boy. They must be yours". Jimmy immediately took the skates and ran home. At his own doorstep he looked back. The boy was still sitting where Jimmy had left him, but now he was leaning over with his head on his arms, crying. Jimmy had thought he would be perfectly happy to have his skates back again. He had been so sorry to lose them. He had hunted high and low for them. But he couldn't help thinking about that little boy. He kept remembering how he had looked, hunched over there on the sidewalk with his head down, crying. Jimmy thought so hard about it that he couldn't enjoy his dinner. As he was getting ready for bed, he suddenly made up his mind. He ran downstairs where his parents were and asked to talk to them. He told them about the boy who had his skates. He also told them how the boy had cried. Jimmy asked his mother if he could give the skates back to the boy. He really believed they were his, and somehow it didn't seem right to take them away just because the trash man had mistakenly thought that they were being thrown away when he found them in the gutter. "I think you are right", said his mother. "And I will tell you something else that I think", as she kissed his forehead, "I think you are a good boy". The next morning, Jimmy and his mother drove over to Stephen's house to give him the skates. Stephen was so happy, and so was Jimmy.

After reading this story, ask the class if it is easy to be kind to someone who has been mean to them. Remind them that if a person has high self-esteem, they will be kind to others.

Have them write the following quotes in their journals:

"Kindness is a language which the deaf can hear and the blind can read" –Mark Twain

"If you want others to be happy, practice compassion. If you want to be happy, practice compassion". – The Dalai Lama

Summarize the lesson by teaching that if we are kind to others we will be happier and have better self-esteem. Others will want to be around us because we treat them well. We will be rewarded in so many ways if we just show more kindness.

Collect all of the journals and Spotlight papers from the students. Pass out each of the Spotlight papers after you have checked to make sure all of the comments are positive.

COURAGE

Objectives
-Spotlight
-Discuss the meaning of Courage
-Drawing activity on Courage
-Role play Courage
-"On a roll" activity
-Play "March Madness"

Materials
-A journal for every student
-3-4 pieces of construction paper for Spotlights
-1 piece of paper and a small book
-1 brown paper bag with a picture of a basketball hoop and the word Courage on the front

Activity A–Spotlight

Tell the students that you are going to start the lesson by doing Spotlight. Pick one journal without letting the students see which one you pick. Read the answers to the Spotlight questions in that journal and see if someone can guess whose answers you've read. You can either have the students stand and then sit when an answer is not theirs, leaving the last person standing, or you can read the answers and at the end, choose a student to guess. After the person is guessed, ask them to come to the front of the class. Ask them more questions about themselves such as pets, siblings, hobbies, etc. Next, ask members of the class to say 5 nice things about this person being Spotlighted. While they are doing this, write the name of the student being Spotlighted in the center of a piece of construction paper. Pass around the sheet and let all students write something positive about that person all over the page. When the paper is done being passed around to each student, you will collect it and give it to the student at the end of the lesson.

Make sure all of the comments are positive before handing back to the student. Also, write the word "Done" on the front of each journal of those you have Spotlighted so you don't repeat. You will Spotlight about 3-4 students during each lesson depending on how many students you have in the class.

Pass out all of the journals

Next, ask the class about the "Kids Catching Kids" jar. See if they participated during the last month in filling out cards and placing them inside the jar. Take a few minutes and read the cards to see how kindness was shown.

Activity B–Discuss the meaning of Courage

Write on the board the letters A, E, O, U, G, C, R. Tell the students that the topic today is spelled with these letters. See who can unscramble the word first. Write Courage on the board with the definition. **Courage is being brave enough to do what you should do even when you're afraid.** Have the students write this in their journals. As a class, brainstorm ideas as to what people might find scary. Talk about how being brave is not easy. Ask the students these questions:

Do I stand up for what is right even if I am the only one who does?
Am I scared to try something new even if it makes me feel afraid?

Lead a discussion and even add your own personal stories of when you used courage in a difficult situation. (Maybe riding a roller coaster or finding a mouse inside your house)

Activity C–Drawing activity on Courage

Have the students tear out a piece of paper from their journals. Have them draw a line down the middle. On the left side, have the students draw a picture of something that scares them. On the right side, have them draw a picture of how they can show courage in that same situation. Allow some students to share if they so choose.

Activity D–Role playing Courage

As a class, brainstorm situations that could occur that might cause fear in the students. Examples could be, someone bullying another student, getting lost in a large place, facing a scary dog, going to the dentist or doctor, seeing a friend steal candy at the store, etc. Have different students come to the front of the class and role play first the negative situation, then the solution. You can make up many different scenarios to role play using courage.

Activity E–"On a roll" activity

Choose a student to come to the front of the class. Show them a piece of paper and a small book. Ask them if there is any way that the paper can hold up the book using no hands. Let them try for a few seconds. Then take the paper and roll it into a tube. Hold it up and place the book on top of the open end of the tube. You should be able to balance it on a desk.

Relate this to the ability we each have of turning our weaknesses into strengths. The paper at first is flimsy, weak, lacking backbone, easy to crush and overwhelm. This might be compared to some people who are faced with a problem or obstacle. They may lack the courage to confront the problem or stand up to the opposition. There are ways we can turn weaknesses into strengths. Through practice, determination, patience, and perseverance, we can improve and sharpen our skills. Just as the paper can be rolled into a sturdy tube, we can work to add muscle to our frailties if we have the courage to persist. We will thereby develop the fortitude and backbone to hold up under pressure. Ask someone in the class to turn the following weaknesses into strengths.

-Tommy has to give a speech in class and is afraid to speak in front of his classmates.

-Jenny loves ice cream and cookies but she has gained 10 pounds in the last year.

-Jeffrey is short for his age but wants to make the basketball team at school.

Activity F–"March Madness"

Make a basketball net by attaching a large brown paper bag to the board with the bag being open. Draw a basketball net on the front of the bag and write "Courage" across the front. Have the students tear out a piece of paper in their journals and write the thing they are most afraid of doing. Let each student call out the fear they came up with, ball it up, and shoot into the net. Tell them this represents facing our fears, overcoming them, and letting go of them.

Have the students write in their journals the following quote.

"Kites rise highest against the wind, not with it". – Winston Churchill

End the lesson by telling the students that Courage comes with trying something new, sometimes failing at it, and then trying again. When we use courage with the hard things and accomplish our goals, then we will have better self-esteem.

Collect all of the journals and Spotlight papers from the students. Pass out each of the Spotlight papers after you have checked to make sure all of the comments are positive.

HUMILITY

Objectives
-Spotlight
-Discuss the meaning of Humility
-Read the story, "The Lion and the Mouse"
-Role play Humility
-Humility worksheet

Materials
-A journal for every student
-3-4 pieces of construction paper for Spotlights
-The story of "The Lion and the Mouse"
-A humility worksheet for every student

Activity A–Spotlight

Tell the students that you are going to start the lesson by doing Spotlight. Pick one journal without letting the students see which one you pick. Read the answers to the Spotlight questions in that journal and see if someone can guess whose answers you've read. You can either have the students stand and then sit when an answer is not theirs, leaving the last person standing, or you can read the answers and at the end, choose a student to guess. After the person is guessed, ask them to come to the front of the class. Ask them more questions about themselves such as pets, siblings, hobbies, etc. Next, ask members of the class to say 5 nice things about this person being Spotlighted. While they are doing this, write the name of the student being Spotlighted in the center of a piece of construction paper. Pass around the sheet and let all students write something positive about that person all over the page. When the paper is done being passed around to each student, you will collect it and give it to the student at the end of the lesson.

Make sure all of the comments are positive before handing back to the student. Also write the word "Done" on the front of each journal of those you have Spotlighted so you don't repeat. You will Spotlight about 3-4 students during each lesson depending on how many are in the class.

Pass out all of the journals

Activity B–Discuss the meaning of Humility

Tell the students that the topic you are going to discuss is Humility. Ask them if they know the definition of Humility. Have them write in their journals, **Humility is putting others first by giving up what you think you deserve.** Tell the class that being humble does not mean you cannot be excited about your accomplishments. Have a few students share something that they are really proud of accomplishing. But then have them tell who helped them achieve this goal, or whom they couldn't have done it without. We have to get in the habit of recognizing those who help us achieve great things. Tell the students that humility does not equal weakness but can actually equal greatness. They should take pleasure in their accomplishments, not pride in them. Humble people recognize their own strengths but have the confidence to recognize greatness in others. "Please" and "Thank You" are important words to use. Let them know that people will help you, depending on your attitude and how you react to them. You can give them some scenarios or have them think of a few examples.

Activity C–Read the story "The Lion and the Mouse"

Read the story to the class then follow up with a discussion.

One day a great lion lay asleep in the sunshine. A little mouse ran across his paw and wakened him. The great lion was just going to eat him up when the mouse cried, "Oh, please, let me go, sir. Some day I may help you."

The lion laughed at the thought that the little mouse could be of any use to him. But he was a good-natured lion, and he set the mouse free.

Not long after, the lion was caught in a net. He tugged and pulled with all his might, but the ropes were too strong. Then he roared loudly. The little mouse heard him, and ran to the spot.

"Be still, dear Lion, and I will set you free. I will gnaw the ropes."

With his sharp little teeth, the mouse cut the ropes, and the lion came out of the net.

"You laughed at me once," said the mouse. "You thought I was too little to do you a good turn. But see, you owe your life to a poor little mouse."

Ask the class if they have ever heard of Aesop's Fables? Aesop was a Greek writer who wrote short stories that teach a lesson. Tell the students that the lion showed humility towards the mouse by letting it go. In return, the mouse saved the lion's life. The moral of the story is that little friends may prove to be a great help! Now ask the students which one of the characters in the story are most like them? The Lion or the Mouse? Why? Ask, "Who could you show humility to this week and how could that be important later on?"

Activity D–Role play Humility

Tell the students that you are going to choose a few of them to act out humility in different situations. Ask for a volunteer to come to the front of the class. Tell them that you are going to give them a situation and you want them to act out their response in two different ways. First, respond in an arrogant manner. Second, respond in a humble manner. Choose new volunteers for each scenario.

Use the following scenarios:
-You just won the spelling bee for the whole school.
-You just found a $100 bill.
-You just got picked to be on the best soccer team.

Discuss the difference between arrogance and humility.

Activity E–Humility worksheet

Pass out a Humility worksheet to every student. Read the directions at the top of the page and then give them a few minutes to complete it. Go around the room and have a few of the students share their answers.

Give a real life example of Humility by reading the following story.

The world's most famous female scientist understood a lot about humility. Marie Curie was an excellent student. When she was 16 years old she graduated at the top of her class. But instead of rushing off to college, Marie worked for six years as a governess to put her older sister through medical school. Later, Marie gave up comforts and luxuries in order to devote herself to research that would help the world and change our understanding of matter and energy. Marie was the first woman to win a Nobel Prize and the only woman to ever win two! Discuss with the class and ask them how Marie Curie showed humility. Ask them to think about what good thing might happen if they decide to put others first by giving up what they think they deserve.

End the lesson by having each student pair up with their neighbor for 2 minutes and ask them to discuss each others strengths. (ex., math, playing sports, art, dance, etc.) Ask the class if they noticed anything that they were both able to do well, and if one of the students was better at something than the other student. They can write in their journals, "I am great at _____, but _____ is better at _____ than I am".

Have them also write the following quotes in their journals.

"The only way to get the best of an argument is to avoid it"-Dale Carnegie

"There is no respect for others without humility in one's self"- Henri Amiel

Challenge the students to remember to be a little more humble at school by giving up their seat, job, snack, prize box visit, etc. for someone else. They will feel better about themselves by being kind to others.

Collect all of the journals and Spotlight papers from the students. Pass out each of the Spotlight papers after you have checked to make sure all of the comments are positive.

Name_____

HUMILITY

Directions: There are many ways we can show humility at school with our friends, and with our family. Fill out this chart and write about how you can be humble when you are doing these things.

When I......	.....I can show humility by......
Am watching TV with my siblings	
Am playing a video game with a friend	
Am going somewhere I don't want to go with my family	
Am eating dinner with my family and there is only one piece of pie left	
Am in my room with a friend who wants to play with a toy I don't want to play with	
Can spend some money on anything I want	
Just bought some candy	
Am playing a game outside with my friends	
Am arguing with my cousin	

FRIENDSHIP

Objectives
-Spotlight
-Discuss the meaning of Friendship
-Read Story about Dolphin
-Silhouette Activity
-Final review of Project Self-Esteem

Materials
-A journal for every student
-3-4 pieces of construction paper for Spotlights
-Butcher paper at least 5 feet long, cut into a silhouette of one of your students.

Activity A–Spotlight

Tell the students that you are going to start the lesson by doing Spotlight. Pick one journal without letting the students see which one you pick. Read the answers to the Spotlight questions in that journal and see if someone can guess whose answers you've read. You can either have the students stand and then sit when an answer is not theirs, leaving the last person standing, or you can read the answers and at the end, choose a student to guess. After the person is guessed, ask them to come to the front of the class. Ask them more questions about themselves such as pets, siblings, hobbies, etc. Next, ask members of the class to say 5 nice things about this person being Spotlighted. While they are doing this, write the name of the student being Spotlighted in the center of a piece of construction paper. Pass around the sheet and let all students write something positive about that person all over the page. When the paper is done being passed around to each student, you will collect it and give it to the student at the end of the lesson. Do this for all remaining students who have not yet had the opportunity this year. **Make sure all of the comments are positive before handing back to the student.**

Pass out all of the journals

Activity B–Discuss the meaning of Friendship

Tell the students that the topic you are going to discuss is Friendship. Ask them if they know the definition. After you have heard a few responses, write the definition on the board and have them copy in their journals. **Friendship is a relationship between two or more people who enjoy each others company and have trust in one another.** Ask the students to think about a time when someone was a friend to them. Spend a little time letting the students share their stories with the class.

Activity C–Read story about Dolphin

Dolphins are very playful mammals. They like to play with other animals like turtles, fish or birds. Dolphins are also known to be good friends with people. There are even stories about Dolphins saving people who were drowning or stranded at sea. Dolphins see with their ears by listening to their own echoes. With this type of radar, they are able to tell the size, shape, speed, distance and direction of other things in the water. Dolphins live in groups called pods, a type of large family. They will defend and take care of each other. When it is time for a baby to be born, other female Dolphins gather to protect them. Since Dolphins are mammals and need oxygen from air and not from water, as fish do, babies must be brought up to the surface to survive. After the birth, the baby must breath right away, so the mother pushes the baby to the surface with the help of other Dolphin friends. Dolphins look out for each other, enjoy one another, and can trust other Dolphins in their time of need.

Activity D–Silhouette Activity

Prepare ahead of time a large piece of butcher paper cut out in the shape of one of the student's silhouettes. Hang the cut out up on the chalkboard. Tell the students that the silhouette is named "Bob". Have them come up one by one and write a mean put down about Bob somewhere on the silhouette **in pencil**. Then after they have completed writing their put down, have them tear off the portion of the silhouette where they wrote and take it back to their seat. When everyone has completed this task, there shouldn't be much of Bob left. Ask the students the following question. What did they do to Bob? Tell them that they literally tore him apart with their put downs. Now have them erase their negative comment and rewrite a positive one and bring their piece of Bob back to the front of the class. One by one, have the students tape him back together until the silhouette of Bob is whole again.

Ask the students to tell you how Bob looks now that he is taped back together. Does he look the same as he did when we first started? They should all see that although he is back in one piece, he is not the same as he was when we began. This represents how negative put downs can hurt a person deep inside. You can say you are sorry, but your harsh words will always leave a mark. Tell the students that before they put down another person or say something unkind, they should think to themselves, "How is what I am about to say going to affect this person"?

In summarizing the lesson, lead a discussion tying in friendship with bullying. Ask the students what they would do if they saw someone being a bully to a friend? To have a good friend, you must be a good friend. Think about what kind of friend you want to be, and if you act upon it, you will have no trouble making great friendships.

Activity E–Final review of Project Self Esteem

Before the lesson, read through the previous lessons from this past year and write down some questions to ask the class about the subjects you have taught.

Explain that they have used their journals to take notes on the lessons you have taught. They may use their notes to answer your questions. To make it more fun, bring prizes for the students to give when then answer your questions correctly. Prizes could be pencils, stickers, snacks, etc.

End the lesson by telling the students that you have enjoyed helping them learn what good self-esteem means. Tell them that they are the only ones that have the greatest opportunity to compliment themselves. This means that they are the ones that create their own Self-Esteem. No one can ultimately make them believe that they are not good enough. They always have the choice to do better and act better. In turn, they will feel good about themselves.

Pass out each of the Spotlight papers after you have checked to make sure all of the comments are positive.

(The journals are for the students to keep.)

RESPECT

Objectives
-Introduce Spotlight
-Discuss the meaning of Respect
-Take Self-Respect Quiz
-Golden Rule Activity
-Chalkboard Activity

Materials
-A journal for every student
-Four 8 ½ X 11 papers for Spotlight
-A Self Respect quiz for every student
-2 Pictures of different kinds of Trees

Activity A–Introduce Facilitator. Project Self-Esteem and Spotlight

Tell the students your name and a little bit about yourself and that you are here to teach Project Self-Esteem. Self-esteem means how you feel about yourself. If you feel good about yourself, you will be happy and treat others well. Explain that your goal is to teach them to have good self-esteem through your lessons each month. Tell them that each one of them is special and this year you are going to find out why.

Pass out a journal to each student and ask them to write their name on the front cover. Tell the students that these journals are for them to take notes in during each of your lessons. Explain that when they take notes, they will better remember what you have taught. They will have their notes to refer to at the last lesson where you will have a review of the entire year. Now have the students open to the first page and write the date and number the lines 1 to 10. Ask the 10 following questions:

1. What is your favorite color?
2. What is your favorite food?
3. What is your favorite restaurant?
4. What is your favorite movie or T.V. show?
5. What is your favorite sport?
6. What is your favorite thing to do in your free time?
7. What is a talent that you have?
8. Where is a place that you would like to visit?
9. What would you like to be when you grow up?
10. Who is a person you admire? (dead or alive)

When you are done asking the questions, tell the students you are going to play a game called Spotlight with them at the end of the lesson. Have them turn to the next page in their journals and tell them they should be taking notes throughout the lesson.

Activity B–Discuss the meaning of Respect

Tell the students that today you are going to discuss the meaning of Respect. Write the word on the board and ask if anyone knows the definition. After answers are given, write the definition on the board and have them copy it in their journals. **Respect is showing others they are important by what you say or do.** People who understand and use respect will be better members of society, better friends, and better leaders. There are many ways to show respect. You show it by how you treat other people and yourself. You have to respect yourself before you can respect others.

Activity C–Take Self-Respect Quiz

Pass out the Self-Respect Quiz to each student. Give them a few minutes to take the quiz. Lead a discussion about the quiz going over each answer. Get feedback from the different students. This should be an interesting conversation and should show how we would all have better self- respect.

Self-Respect Quiz

Which actions show self-respect and which do not?

Directions: Write "yes" on the chart below if these actions show self-respect. If the action does not show self-respect, write why.

Action	Does this show self-respect?	If not, why?
Reading every day		
Eating candy for breakfast		
Trying your hardest at sports		
Doing homework right away		
Picking fights with others		
Watching t.v. for 5 hrs a day		
Helping your mother at home		
Putting down your friends		
Cheating on tests		
Stealing money		
Scaring little children		
Collecting baseball cards		
Being with people who take drugs		
Doing your chores		
Not trying during P.E.		
Not ever eating lunch		
Helping out someone in need		
Playing video games all day		

Activity D–Golden rule activity

Bring from home a picture of a tree in nature and a Christmas tree (decorated). Begin by choosing 2 students to come to the front of the class. Have them stand facing each other approximately 6 feet apart. Bring out the pictures of the 2 trees (1 tree on each side) and hold between them so that each person is looking at a different side. **Tell them that you have a picture of the same item on both sides of the poster.** Ask the two students to take turns describing one feature of the object they see without telling what the object is to the others. Examples would be it has leaves, its green, its brown, its tall, etc. After both have responded, and they begin to realize they are talking about different things, ask them why there might be a discrepancy between the two views. Ask one of them how they might resolve this disagreement. Ask one of them the following possibilities. 1. Tell the other person they are wrong. 2. Argue with him and insist that your description is correct. 3. Come around to the other side and try to see the picture from the other persons point of view.

Hopefully the students will decide the third choice is the wisest. Have one of the students walk around and look at the other tree. Then ask the students the following questions:

1. Why is it important to see things from the other person's point of view?
2. Why do people often argue about something instead of attempting to see the other side?
3. What is the Golden Rule and what does it teach us to do?
4. Does the Golden Rule help us avoid arguments? How?

Can you think of a time you knew you were right about something and someone disagreed with you? How did you resolve it? Were you willing to listen to the other person's opinion and try to see it from his standpoint?

Activity E–Make a Respect Chart on chalkboard

Make a chart on the chalkboard with the heading saying **RESPECT CHART.** Under this heading, write on the left side of the board **WHO/WHAT**, and on the right side write **HOW.**

RESPECT CHART

WHO/WHAT   **HOW**

This chart helps the students PLAN to be respectful. Using the left-hand column, ask the students to list categories of people and things that deserve respect. As you list them one at a time, discuss how respect for that person or thing can be given effectively.

Activity F–Spotlight

Collect all of the journals. Pick one journal without letting the students see which one you pick. Read the answers to the Spotlight questions in that journal and see if someone can guess whose answers you've read. You can either have the students stand and then sit when an answer is not theirs, leaving the last student standing, or you can read the answers and at the end choose a student to guess. After the person is guessed, ask them to come to the front of the class. Ask them more questions about themselves such as pets, siblings, hobbies, etc. Next, ask members of the class to say 5 nice things about this person being Spotlighted. While they're doing this, write the name of the student being Spotlighted in the center of a piece of construction paper. Pass around the sheet and let all of the students write something positive about that person all over the page. When the paper is done being passed around to each student, you will collect it and give it to the student.

Make sure all of the comments are positive before handing back to the student. Also, write the word "Done" on the front of each journal of those you have Spotlighted so you don't repeat. You will Spotlight about 3-4 students during each lesson depending on how many are in the class.

Tell the class that these Spotlight papers are for them to keep in a safe place. If they are having a bad day and not feeling good about themselves, then they can get out this paper and see the positive comments that were made about them. This should raise their self-esteem!

UNIQUENESS

Objectives

-Spotlight
-Discuss the meaning of Uniqueness
-Take the "Preference Profile sheet" Quiz
-Play the "Special Me" Game
-Object lesson on Uniqueness

Materials

-A journal for every student
-3-4 pieces of construction paper for Spotlights
-A copy of the "Preference Profile sheet" quiz for every student

Activity A–Spotlight

Tell the students that you are going to start the lesson by doing Spotlight. Pick one journal without letting the students see which one you pick. Read the answers to the Spotlight questions in that journal and see if someone can guess whose answers you've read. You can either have the students stand and then sit when an answer is not theirs, leaving the last person standing, or you can read the answers and at the end, choose a student to guess. After the person is guessed, ask them to come to the front of the class. Ask them more questions about themselves such as pets, siblings, hobbies, etc. Next, ask members of the class to say 5 nice things about this person being Spotlighted. While they are doing this, write the name of the student being Spotlighted in the center of a piece of construction paper. Pass around the sheet and let all students write something positive about that person all over the page. When the paper is done being passed around to each student, you will collect it and give it to the student at the end of the lesson.

Make sure all of the comments are positive before handing back to the student. Also, write the word "Done" on the front of each journal of those you have Spotlighted so you don't repeat. You will Spotlight about 3-4 students during each lesson depending on how many are in the class.

Pass out all of the journals.

Activity B–Discuss the meaning of Uniqueness

Tell the students that today you are going to talk about being unique. Ask if anyone knows the definition of Uniqueness. After choosing a few responses, write the definition on the board and have the students copy in their journals. **Uniqueness is learning more about others so you can know more about yourself.** As a class, discuss the importance of being an individual. One uses their individual talents to make a difference in the world. Discuss what it would be like if we all looked the same, acted the same, and had the same talents in the world. BORING!!! Have the students write in their journals, "I am different because I........." Some of them might like to share their responses.

Activity C–Take the "Preference Profile sheet" Quiz

Pass out to each student the "Preference Profile Sheet" Quiz. Tell them that you will give them a few minutes to complete the quiz. After they are done, ask for volunteers to share some of their answers. This activity will show that students might have different responses to situations and that is what makes them unique.

Activity D–Play the "Special Me" Game

Have each student tear out a piece of paper from their journals. Have them write their name on one side. Collect all of the papers and then pass them out so no one gets their own name. Tell them to write a compliment about that person such as, "beautiful hair, best dressed, very athletic, etc." Have them think of unique things to say about that person. Collect the papers and put them into a hat or jar. Take out each slip of paper and read the compliment and have the class guess who the student is being described.

Activity E–Object lesson on Uniqueness

Discuss Thanksgiving and how the Pilgrims and Indians each brought unique foods and traditions to the first Thanksgiving. Take turns and let a few students share what their family does to celebrate Thanksgiving. Topics to share would be things such as foods that are eaten, and activities that are done. Have each student take off their left shoe and make a line with them in the center of the room. Discuss all the similarities the shoes have and that they all serve the same basic purpose. Then discuss all the unique qualities about each shoe and that those qualities add to the character of the shoe.

Display the following quotes and have the students write them in their journals.

"Always be a first-rate version of yourself, instead of a second-rate version of somebody else." – Judy Garland

"There is just one life for each of us: our own."- Euripides

End the lesson by telling the students that each one of them is unique and that they should appreciate themselves and others for being unique. Just because they might think others are different, that doesn't mean they should make fun of them or be mean to them. When we have good self-esteem, we are kind to others.

Collect all of the journals and Spotlight papers from the students. Pass out each of the Spotlight papers after you have checked to make sure all of the comments are positive.

Name_____

Preference Profile Sheet

Read each of the pairs of statements below and circle the answer that most describes your preference. Please circle one answer in every pair.

    If you have difficulty choosing between two answers, circle the answer that is most true for you most of the time.

1. Like to work alone   Like to work with others

2. Morning person   Night person

3. Work by plan   Work in bursts of energy

4. Enjoy routine   Like change

5. Can do several things at once   Need to focus

6. Can see both sides of most issues   Need to take a stand

7. Prefer to eat and sleep on schedule   Eat when hungry/sleep when tired

8. Like music when studying   Prefer quiet when studying

9. Like to work at a desk   Prefer to work on bed or armchair

10. Have a way with animals   Don't care much about animals

11. Like vivid colors   Prefer quiet colors

12. Enjoy a variety of foods   Like to stick with favorite foods

J O Y

Objectives
-Spotlight
-Play Pictionary and discuss the meaning of Joy
-Drawing activity on Joy
-Object lesson on Joy
-Make Joy Lists and Joy promise cards

Materials
-A journal for every student
-3-4 pieces of construction paper for Spotlights
-Slips of paper with the words: smile, laugh, party, and happy
-A 3x5 card for every student

Activity A–Spotlight

Tell the students that you are going to start the lesson by doing Spotlight. Pick one journal without letting the students see which one you pick. Read the answers to the Spotlight questions in that journal and see if someone can guess whose answers you've read. You can either have the students stand and then sit when an answer is not theirs, leaving the last person standing, or you can read the answers and at the end, choose a student to guess. After the person is guessed, ask them to come to the front of the class. Ask them more questions about themselves such as pets, siblings, hobbies, etc. Next, ask members of the class to say 5 nice things about this person being Spotlighted. While they are doing this, write the name of the student being Spotlighted in the center of a piece of construction paper. Pass around the sheet and let all students write something positive about that person all over the page. When the paper is done being passed around to each student, you will collect it and give it to the student at the end of the lesson.

Make sure all of the comments are positive before handing back to the student. Also, write the word "Done" on the front of each journal of those you have Spotlighted so you don't repeat. You will Spotlight about 3-4 students during each lesson depending on how many are in the class.

Pass out all of the journals.

Activity B–Play Pictionary and discuss the meaning of Joy

Tell the students that you are going to have them guess your topic today with the game of Pictionary. Let one student at a time come to the chalkboard to draw a picture. The rest of the class will guess what they are drawing. Use the word strips that say smile, laugh, party, and happy. Once the words have all been guessed, ask the students what all of the words have in common. Their guesses should lead you to the word JOY. Have them write the definition of joy in their journals. **Joy is finding a way to be happy, even when things don't go your way.** Tell them that joy is more than being happy. It's an attitude that one can share with others around them. Joy is not in things; it is in us.

Activity C–Drawing Joy

Tell the students to draw in their journals a picture of a smiley face while looking at the ceiling. When they are done, have them look at the pictures and discuss if they came out the way they had envisioned. Now have them draw the same picture, but let them look at their paper this time. Discuss the differences between the two pictures. The one that the students focused on has the desired outcome. Joy is the same way. When we focus on being happy, even when something isn't going our way, we will have a pleasant outcome: JOY!!

Activity D–Object lesson on Joy

Set up a simple obstacle course (for example, walking around a chair, jumping over a book, hopping on one foot). Demonstrate and then let students try it. Now allow partners to complete the course while holding hands or with their hands on the shoulders of their partner. When you are done with the obstacle course, talk about the differences. Which way is easier? Which way was better? Explain that joy is something that affects others.

Activity E–Make Joy lists

Have the students write in their journals the letters J O Y. Then make a list of words that begin with these letters. Once they have made a list of at least ten words for each letter, have them circle the words that make them feel Joy. Then have them list the Top 10 things that make them happy. Have some of the students share their lists with the class.

Ask the question to the class, "Is it always easy to be happy?" Give them some scenarios where it might be hard to have joy. Some examples might be; failing a test, getting yelled at by an adult, being gossiped about, losing something you really loved, etc. Tell them that they always have a choice in life to be happy or unhappy. It is up to them! Pass out the 3x5 card to each student. Tell the students that they are going to make a joy promise card. Have them write a statement that will remind them to work at being happy even if things don't go their way. Let them sign their name on the bottom or back, then keep it in their backpacks or desks to remind themselves to look for joy in every situation.

Summarize the lesson by telling the students that having joy is an important part of life. When we are happy, we want to do more for others and that will increase our joy and our self-esteem. Joy is contagious. We want to find joy in all we do. Even if things aren't going the way you plan, you can always look on the bright side! This will raise your self-esteem.

Collect all of the journals and Spotlight papers from the students. Pass out each of the Spotlight papers after you have checked to make sure all of the comments are positive.

DETERMINATION

Objectives
-Spotlight
-Discuss the meaning of Determination
-Read the story about Tony Hawk
-Discuss goals and make New Year's resolutions
-Object lesson "Knockout"

Materials
-A journal for every student
-3-4 pieces of construction paper for Spotlights
-Slips of paper with the definition of the word Determination
-Story of Tony Hawk
-A Goal setting sheet for each student
-Empty shoe boxes and post-it notes

Activity A–Spotlight

Tell the students that you are going to start the lesson by doing Spotlight. Pick one journal without letting the students see which one you pick. Read the answers to the Spotlight questions in that journal and see if someone can guess whose answers you've read. You can either have the students stand and then sit when an answer is not theirs, leaving the last person standing, or you can read the answers and at the end, choose a student to guess. After the person is guessed, ask them to come to the front of the class. Ask them more questions about themselves such as pets, siblings, hobbies, etc. Next, ask members of the class to say 5 nice things about this person being Spotlighted. While they are doing this, write the name of the student being Spotlighted in the center of a piece of construction paper. Pass around the sheet and let all students write something positive about that person all over the page. When the paper is done being passed around to each student, you will collect it and give it to the student at the end of the lesson.

Make sure all of the comments are positive before handing back to the student. Also, write the word "Done" on the front of each journal of those you have Spotlighted so you don't repeat. You will Spotlight about 3-4 students during each lesson depending on how many are in the class.

Pass out all of the journals.

Activity B–Discuss the meaning of Determination

Tell the students that today you are going to discuss the meaning of Determination. Tell the class that you have the definition of determination and that you have split it into 9 parts. Choose 9 students to come up to the front of the class and put the definition in the correct order. Have the class write the definition in their journals once it is correct. **Determination is deciding it's worth it to finish what you've started.** Ask the students if they have ever started something but didn't finish it. This could be, not finishing a book, starting Piano lessons but dropping out, etc. Discuss how they felt when they first started (they would feel excitement and eagerness). Then discuss what it was that made them quit. Write the word determination on the board. Have the students think of synonyms of the word such as courage, bravery, will power, etc. After a few minutes, allow the students time to share some of their answers. Add their answers underneath the word "Determination" on the board.

Activity C–Read the story about Tony Hawk

Tony Hawk got his first skateboard when he was 9 years old. Five years later, when was 14, he turned pro. His autobiography and video games have been best sellers, while his foundation has funded skate-park construction in low-income communities across America.

When he was 17, a high school teacher of his scolded him in front of the entire class for jumping ahead in his work book. He told him that he would never make it in the work place if he didn't follow directions explicitly. He said he would never make a living as a skateboarder.

Even during those dark years, he never stopped riding his skateboard and never stopped progressing as a skater. There were many times when he was frustrated because he couldn't land a maneuver. But he realized that the only way to master something was to keep at it. Despite the bloody knees, the twisted ankles, and the mocking crowds, he set his goal to succeed. Tony Hawk's wisdom for young people is to find the thing you love and work hard to succeed at it.

Activity D–Discuss goals and make New Year's resolutions

In January people usually make New Year's resolutions. Discuss how keeping these resolutions can take a lot of determination. Have the students decide on a New Year's resolution they can set for themselves. Have them write these in their journals. You can have a few students share with the class their ideas. Remind them to keep track of their resolutions and not get discouraged if they get off track. Tell them that they should always be working on goals in their lives. Some might be small and some might be big. They will have better self-esteem when they accomplish a goal. Pass out a goal setting sheet to every student and tell them that when they have a plan and write down their goals, they are more likely to accomplish them. Give them a minute or two to fill out the "Goal" sheet

Name_____

GOAL SETTING

Set Reachable Goals.
Write out steps for reaching that goal.
Keep going until you reach your goal.
Give yourself a reasonable time limit.
Evaluate – Check your progress.
Compliment yourself.

My Goal is _____

1		
2		
3		
4		

Activity E—Object lesson "Knockout"

Choose a student to come to the front of the class. Ask them to share a goal that they would like to achieve. Write the goal on a post-it note and stick it to the wall. Next, discuss the things that would prevent them from accomplishing that goal. Write these obstacles on a few post-it notes and stick them on various boxes. Let the student stack the boxes to form a wall between them and the goal. Now, discuss the student's special skills that will help them overcome their doubts or fears in accomplishing their goal. These can be things like creativity, positive thinking, quick learner, etc. As you talk, write these qualities on a post-it note and put it on the student's shirt. Talk about the fact that by having these special skills, the student can accomplish almost anything they set their mind to do. Tell them to face the barricade of boxes and with all their strength, break through. This activity can really give the student a sense of what it feels like to take action in accomplishing their goals.

Summarize the lesson by telling the students that with hard work and determination they can accomplish anything. Even if they fail at something they will learn from it, and if they keep trying they will eventually achieve even hard things. Their self-esteem will improve along the way.

Collect all of the journals and Spotlight papers from the class. Pass out each of the Spotlight papers after you have checked to make sure all of the comments are positive.

KINDNESS

Objectives
-Spotlight
-Discuss the meaning of Kindness
-Introduce "Kids Catching Kids" Jar
-Make kindness cards
-A "Spoonful of Sugar" object lesson
-Read the story, "The Lost Skates"

Materials
-A journal for every student
-3-4 pieces of construction paper for Spotlights
-A jar labeled "Kids Catching Kids" with 3X5 cards inside
-1 piece of paper for each student
-Bring from home a clear glass or bowl, a pepper shaker, 1 tsp sugar, and a bar of soap

Activity A–Spotlight

Tell the students that you are going to start the lesson by doing Spotlight. Pick one journal without letting the students see which one you pick. Read the answers to the Spotlight questions in that journal and see if someone can guess whose answers you've read. You can either have the students stand and then sit when an answer is not theirs, leaving the last person standing, or you can read the answers and at the end, choose a student to guess. After the person is guessed, ask them to come to the front of the class. Ask them more questions about themselves such as pets, siblings, hobbies, etc. Next, ask members of the class to say 5 nice things about this person being Spotlighted. While they are doing this, write the name of the student being Spotlighted in the center of a piece of construction paper. Pass around the sheet and let all students write something positive about that person all over the page. When the paper is done being passed around to each student, you will collect it and give it to the student at the end of the lesson. Do this for 3-4 students.

Make sure all of the comments are positive before handing back to the student. Also, write the word "Done" on the front of each journal of those you have Spotlighted so you don't repeat. You will Spotlight about 3-4 students during each lesson depending on how many are in the class.

Pass out all of the journals

Activity B–Discuss the meaning of Kindness

Write the word Kindness on the board along with the definition. **Kindness is showing others they are valuable by how you treat them.** Have the students copy the definition in their journals. Discuss with the class how it makes them feel when someone is kind to them. Have a few students share examples or situations when someone showed kindness to them and discuss how it made them feel. Talk about the "Golden Rule", which is to do unto others what you would have done unto you. We do not need to take advantage of other people, or call other people names. Compare and contrast showing kindness with actions and just speaking kindness with words.

Activity C–Introduce the "Kids Catching Kids" jar

Show the students the jar labeled "Kids Catching Kids" and tell them that when they catch anyone in their class showing kindness, they are to write it down on a card and put it in the jar. Tell them that at the next project self-esteem lesson, the cards will be read out loud. Discuss ways that they can show kindness to other people outside their normal circle of friends. Discuss how other people possibly do not have as much as they do, and think of ways they could help them. Discuss random acts of kindness. Ask them how it makes them feel when they are kind to someone. (Happy, higher self-esteem, it makes them want to give more, etc.)

Activity D–Make kindness cards

Pass out a piece of paper to each student. Give them a few minutes to make a card for someone. Tell them to write a kind message to someone they admire. Tell them that this small act of kindness will make someone else very happy.

Activity E–"A Spoonful of Sugar" object lesson

Take out a clear glass or bowl and fill it with water. Sprinkle pepper liberally on the water. Tell the class that the pepper represents the people around them. This could be friends, family, teachers, etc. Discuss the fact that how we get along with those people is largely determined by how we treat and speak to them. Words can be very powerful tools, either for good or bad. And it is important to learn positive and kind ways of speaking to our friends. Now talk about an example of someone who does not use kind words when speaking to others. Tell the students that the bar of soap represents negative, harsh language. Have a student touch the soap to the center of the water. The soap will repel the pepper and will cause it to be dispersed to the sides of the bowl. Make the comparison that when we speak unkindly to others, they won't want to be around us, and will want to scatter. Take a tsp of sugar and pour it in the center of the water. Compare the sugar to the sweetness of kind and thoughtful words. Talk about how being loving toward other people usually causes them to be drawn to us, and makes them want to be our friends. They will see how the sugar attracts the pepper back from the sides of the bowl.

Activity F–Read the story, "The Lost Skates"

Tell the class that you are going to read them a short story on Kindness

One afternoon Jimmy was sitting on the front porch, thinking about his lost skates. He was thinking about them because down the street, a little boy was skating back and forth. Watching this boy had made Jimmy think about his own skates. The boy went slowly up and down the street. He seemed to be just learning how to skate. As Jimmy came close, he was surprised to see that the boy's skates looked quite new. "They are just like mine", Jimmy thought. Just then, the boy skated past him and Jimmy saw printed on the straps the word "Jimmy". "Why, those are my skates!" shouted Jimmy. He stepped in front of the boy and stopped him. "Where did you get my skates?" he demanded.

The little boy stared at him with round, frightened eyes. "They're not your skates", he said, "They're mine". "The trash man gave them to me".

"I don't care who gave them to you", said Jimmy crossly, "They are mine". "What is your name?" asked Jimmy.

"Stephen", said the little boy.

"Well! See my name is Jimmy, and it is written right here. I printed it myself, Jimmy. So they are mine", said Jimmy.

The little boy looked worried. "The trash man gave them to me. He found them in the gutter when they had been thrown away".

"They must have rolled down the walk when I took them off", said Jimmy. He recalled the day when he fell down and hurt his cheek. "Well, anyway, I didn't throw them away. And they are mine. Give them to me!"

The little boy sat down and began to tug obediently at the straps. "I guess you're right", said the little boy. "They must be yours".

Jimmy immediately took the skates and ran home. At his own doorstep he looked back. The boy was still sitting where Jimmy had left him, but now he was leaning over with his head on his arms, crying. Jimmy had thought he would be perfectly happy to have his skates back again. He had been so sorry to lose them. He had hunted high and low for them. But he couldn't help thinking about that little boy. He kept remembering how he had looked, hunched over there on the sidewalk with his head down, crying.

Jimmy thought so hard about it that he couldn't enjoy his dinner. As he was getting ready for bed, he suddenly made up his mind. He ran downstairs where his parents were and asked to talk to them. He told them about the boy who had his skates. He also told them how the boy had cried. Jimmy asked his mother if he could give the skates back to the boy. He really believed they were his, and somehow it didn't seem right to take them away just because the trash man had mistakenly thought that they were being thrown away when he found them in the gutter.

"I think you are right", said his mother. "And I will tell you something else that I think", as she kissed his forehead, "I think you are a good boy". The next morning, Jimmy and his mother drove over to Stephen's house to give him the skates. Stephen was so happy, and so was Jimmy.

After reading this story, ask the class if it is easy to be kind to someone who has been mean to them. Remind them that if a person has high self-esteem, they will be kind to others.

Have them write the following quotes in their journals:

"Kindness is a language which the deaf can hear and the blind can read" –Mark Twain

"If you want others to be happy, practice compassion. If you want to be happy, practice compassion". – The Dalai Lama

Summarize the lesson by teaching that if we are kind to others we will be happier and have better self-esteem. Others will want to be around us because we treat them well. We will be rewarded in so many ways if we just show more kindness.

Collect all of the journals and Spotlight papers from the class. Pass out each of the Spotlight papers after you have checked to make sure all of the comments are positive.

COURAGE

Objectives
-Spotlight
-Discuss the meaning of Courage and Bullying
-Drawing activity on Courage
-9/11 Story of Courage
-"On a roll" activity
-Play "March Madness"

Materials
-A journal for every student
-3-4 pieces of construction paper for Spotlights
-1 piece of paper and a small book
-1 brown paper bag with a picture of a basketball hoop on the front

Activity A–Spotlight

Tell the students that you are going to start the lesson by doing Spotlight. Pick one journal without letting the students see which one you pick. Read the answers to the Spotlight questions in that journal and see if someone can guess whose answers you've read. You can either have the students stand and then sit when an answer is not theirs, leaving the last person standing, or you can read the answers and at the end, choose a student to guess. After the person is guessed, ask them to come to the front of the class. Ask them more questions about themselves such as pets, siblings, hobbies, etc. Next, ask members of the class to say 5 nice things about this person being Spotlighted. While they are doing this, write the name of the student being Spotlighted in the center of a piece of construction paper. Pass around the sheet and let all students write something positive about that person all over the page. When the paper is done being passed around to each student, you will collect it and give it to the student at the end of the lesson.

Make sure all of the comments are positive before handing back to the student. Also, write the word "Done" on the front of each journal of those you have Spotlighted so you don't repeat. You will Spotlight about 3-4 students during each lesson depending on how many are in the class.

Pass out all of the journals

Next, ask the class about the "Kids Catching Kids" jar. See if they participated during the last month in filling out cards and placing them inside the jar. Take a few minutes and read the cards to see how kindness was shown.

Activity B–Discuss the meaning of Courage and Bullying

Write on the board the letters A, E, O, U, G, C, R. Tell the students that the topic today is spelled with these letters. See who can unscramble the word first. Write Courage on the board with the definition. **Courage is being brave enough to do what you should do even when you're afraid.** Have the students write this in their journals. As a class, brainstorm ideas as to what people might find scary. Talk about how being brave is not easy. Ask the students these questions:

Do I stand up for what is right even if I am the only one who does?
Am I scared to try something new even if it makes me feel afraid?

Lead a discussion and even add your own personal stories of when you used courage in a difficult situation. (Maybe riding a roller coaster or finding a mouse inside your house)

Next, tell the class that there are those who think they're courageous by pushing others around. This is called being a bully. Bullying is when a person hurts or scares another person on purpose and the person being bullied has a hard time defending himself. Discuss this subject further and end with the students knowing that a bully has low self-esteem. Finish the discussion by helping students understand what they can do if they are bullied or see someone else being bullied and how standing up to a bully takes courage.

Activity C–Drawing activity on Courage

Have the students tear out a piece of paper from their journals. Have them draw a line down the middle. On the left side, have the students draw a picture of something that scares them. On the right side, have them draw a picture of how they can show courage in that same situation. Allow some students to share if they so choose.

Activity D–9/11 Story of Courage

Tell the students that you are going to read what courageous people did after the attack on the United States on September 11, 2001. Almost as soon as the World Trade Center's twin towers fell on 9/11, thousands of firefighters, police officers, construction workers, search and rescue dogs and volunteers headed to Ground Zero to look for survivors. Because they didn't know how many people were trapped alive in the wreckage, firefighters and other rescue workers had to search carefully through the unstable piles of rubble for air pockets called "Voids". They were looking for people who had been unable to escape from the collapsing buildings. To be safe, they didn't use any heavy equipment at first. Some dug with their bare hands, while others formed bucket brigades to move small amounts of debris as efficiently as possible. Unfortunately, there were not many survivors to find. Two firemen were pulled from their truck in a cavity beneath some wreckage, and a few people were pinned at the edges of the pile. By September 12th, workers had rescued all of the people who were trapped at the site. After that, the Ground Zero workers had a new and more heartbreaking mission. It was to sift carefully through the debris in search of human remains. The fallen buildings were unstable, and engineers worried that the weight of trucks and cranes would cause the wreckage to shift and collapse again. Meanwhile, huge fires continued to burn in the center of the pile. The work was so dangerous that many firefighters and police officers wrote their names and phone numbers on their forearms in case they fell into the hole or were crushed.

This is just a small insight into the nightmare that was 9/11. It took so much courage for the rescue workers to save lives and find others not so fortunate. Ask the class to imagine that time, and would they have been as courageous as the rescuers.

Activity E–"On a roll" activity

Choose a student to come to the front of the class. Show them a piece of paper and a small book. Ask them if there is any way that the paper can hold up the book using no hands. Let them try for a few seconds. Then take the paper and roll it into a tube. Hold it up and place the book on top of the open end of the tube. You should be able to balance it on a desk.

Relate this to the ability we each have of turning our weaknesses into strengths. The paper at first is flimsy, weak, lacking backbone, easy to crush and overwhelm. This might be compared to some people who are faced with a problem or obstacle. They may lack the courage to confront the problem or stand up to the opposition. There are ways we can turn weaknesses into strengths. Through practice, determination, patience, and perseverance, we can improve and sharpen our skills. Just as the paper can be rolled into a sturdy tube, we can work to add muscle to our frailties if we have the courage to persist. We will thereby develop the fortitude and backbone to hold up under pressure. Ask someone in the class to turn the following weaknesses into strengths.

-Tommy has to give a speech in class and is afraid to speak in front of his classmates.
-Jenny loves ice cream and cookies but she has gained 10 pounds in the last year.
-Jeffrey is short for his age but wants to make the basketball team at school.

Activity F–"March Madness"

Make a basketball net by attaching a large brown paper bag to the board with the bag being open. Draw a basketball net on the front of the bag and write "Courage" across the front. Have the students tear out a piece of paper in their journals and write the thing they are most afraid of doing. Let each student call out the fear they came up with, ball it up, and shoot into the net. Tell them this represents facing our fears, overcoming them, and letting go of them.

Have the students write in their journals the following quote;

"Kites rise highest against the wind, not with it". – Winston Churchill

End the lesson by telling the students that Courage comes with trying something new, sometimes failing at it, and then trying again. When a person experiences something that takes courage, they will raise their self-esteem as they accomplish it.

Collect all of the journals and Spotlight papers from the students. Pass out the Spotlight papers after you have made sure that all comments are positive.

H U M I L I T Y

Objectives
-Spotlight
-Discuss the meaning of Humility
-Role play Humility
-Read the story, "The Lion and the Mouse"
-Humility worksheet

Materials
-A journal for every student
-3-4 pieces of construction paper for Spotlight
-The story of "The Lion and the Mouse"
-A humility worksheet for every student

Activity A–Spotlight

Tell the students that you are going to start the lesson by doing Spotlight. Pick one journal without letting the students see which one you pick. Read the answers to the Spotlight questions in that journal and see if someone can guess whose answers you've read. You can either have the students stand and then sit when an answer is not theirs, leaving the last person standing, or you can read the answers and at the end, choose a student to guess. After the person is guessed, ask them to come to the front of the class. Ask them more questions about themselves such as pets, siblings, hobbies, etc. Next, ask members of the class to say 5 nice things about this person being Spotlighted. While they are doing this, write the name of the student being Spotlighted in the center of a piece of construction paper. Pass around the sheet and let all students write something positive about that person all over the page. When the paper is done being passed around to each student, you will collect it and give it to the student at the end of the lesson.

Make sure all of the comments are positive before handing back to the student. Also, write the word "Done" on the front of each journal of those you have Spotlighted so you don't repeat. You will Spotlight about 3-4 students during each lesson depending on how many are in the class.

Pass out all of the journals

Activity B–Discuss the meaning of Humility

Tell the students that the topic you are going to discuss is Humility. Ask them if they know the definition. Have them write in their journals, **Humility is putting others first by giving up what you think you deserve.** Tell the class that being humble does not mean you cannot be excited about your accomplishments. Have a few students share something that they are really proud of accomplishing. Then have them tell who helped them achieve this goal, or who they couldn't have done it without. We have to get in the habit of recognizing those who help us achieve great things. Tell the students that humility does not equal weakness but can actually equal greatness. They should take pleasure in their accomplishments, not pride in them. Humble people recognize their own strengths, but have the confidence to recognize greatness in others. "Please" and "Thank You" are important words to use. Let them know that people will help you depending on your attitude and how you react to them. You can give them some scenarios or have them think of a few examples.

Activity C–Role play Humility

Tell the students that you are going to choose a few of them to act out humility in different situations. Ask for a volunteer to come to the front of the class. Tell them that you are going to give them a situation and you want them to act out their response in two different ways. First, respond in an arrogant manner. Second, respond in a humble manner. Change volunteers for example scenario.

Use the following scenarios:

-You just won the spelling bee for the whole school.
-You just found a $100 bill.
-You just got picked to be on the best soccer team.

End this discussion by showing the difference between arrogance and humility.

Activity D–Read the story "The Lion and the Mouse"

Read the story to the class then follow up with a discussion.

One day a great lion lay asleep in the sunshine. A little mouse ran across his paw and wakened him. The great lion was just going to eat him up when the mouse cried, "Oh, please, let me go, sir. Some day I may help you."

The lion laughed at the thought that the little mouse could be of any use to him. But he was a good-natured lion, and he set the mouse free.

Not long after, the lion was caught in a net. He tugged and pulled with all his might, but the ropes were too strong. Then he roared loudly. The little mouse heard him, and ran to the spot.

"Be still, dear Lion, and I will set you free. I will gnaw the ropes."

With his sharp little teeth, the mouse cut the ropes, and the lion came out of the net.

"You laughed at me once," said the mouse. "You thought I was too little to do you a good turn. But see, you owe your life to a poor little mouse."

Ask the class if they have ever heard of Aesop's Fables? Aesop was a Greek writer who wrote short stories that teach a lesson. Tell the students that the lion showed humility towards the mouse by letting it go. In return, the mouse saved the lion's life. The moral of the story is that little friends may prove to be a great help! Now ask the students which one of the characters in the story are most like them? The Lion or the Mouse? Why? Ask, "Who could you show humility to this week and how could that be important later on?"

Activity E—Humility Worksheet

Pass out a Humility worksheet to every student. Read the directions at the top of the page and then give them a few minutes to complete it. Go around the room and have a few of the students share their answers.

Name_____

HUMILITY

Directions: There are many ways we can show humility at school with our friends, and with our family. Fill out this chart and write about how you can be humble when you are doing these things.

When I......	**.....I can show humility by......**
Am watching TV with my siblings	
Am playing a video game with a friend	
Am going somewhere I don't want to go with my family	
Am eating dinner with my family and there is only one piece of pie left	
Am in my room with a friend who wants to play with a toy I don't want to play with	
Can spend some money on anything I want	
Just bought some candy	
Am playing a game outside with my friends	
Am arguing with my cousin	

Give a real life example of Humility by reading the following story.

The world's most famous female scientist understood a lot about humility. Marie Curie was an excellent student. When she was 16 years old she graduated at the top of her class. But instead of rushing off to college, Marie worked for six years as a governess to put her older sister through medical school. Later, Marie gave up comforts and luxuries in order to devote herself to research that would help the world and change our understanding of matter and energy. Marie was the first woman to win a Nobel Prize and the only woman to ever win two! Discuss with the class and ask them how Marie Curie showed humility. Ask them to think about what good thing might happen if they decide to put others first by giving up what they think they deserve.

End the lesson by having each student pair up with their neighbor for 2 minutes and ask them to discuss each others strengths. (Things they do well, ex., math, playing sports, art, dance, etc.) Ask the class if they noticed anything that they were both able to do well, and if one of the students was better at something than the other student. They can write in their journals, "I am great at _____, but _____ is better at _____ than I am".

Have them also write the following quotes in their journals.

"The only way to get the best of an argument is to avoid it"-Dale Carnegie

"There is no respect for others without humility in one's self"- Henri Amiel

Challenge the students to remember to be a little more humble at school by giving up their seat, job, snack, prize box visit, etc. for someone else. They will feel better about themselves by being kind to others and in turn this will raise their self-esteem.

Collect all of the journals and Spotlight papers from the students. Pass out the Spotlight papers after you have made sure that all comments are positive.

F R I E N D S H I P

Objectives
-Spotlight
-Discuss the meaning of Friendship
-Friendship Circle
-Read Story about Dolphin
-Silhouette Activity

Materials
-A journal for every student
-Enough construction paper to finish Spotlights
-Butcher paper at least 5 feet long, cut into a silhouette of one of your students.

Activity A–Spotlight

Tell the students that you are going to start the lesson by doing Spotlight. Pick one journal without letting the students see which one you pick. Read the answers to the Spotlight questions in that journal and see if someone can guess whose answers you've read. You can either have the students stand and then sit when an answer is not theirs, leaving the last person standing, or you can read the answers and at the end, choose a student to guess. After the person is guessed, ask them to come to the front of the class. Ask them more questions about themselves such as pets, siblings, hobbies, etc. Next, ask members of the class to say 5 nice things about this person being Spotlighted. While they are doing this, write the name of the student being Spotlighted in the center of a piece of construction paper. Pass around the sheet and let all students write something positive about that person all over the page. When the paper is done being passed around to each student, you will collect it and give it to the student at the end of the lesson. Do this for all remaining students who have not yet had the opportunity this year. **Make sure all of the comments are positive before handing back to the student.**

Pass out all of the journals

Activity B–Discuss the meaning of Friendship

Tell the students that the topic you are going to discuss is Friendship. Ask them if they know the definition. After you have heard a few responses, have them write the meaning in their journals. **Friendship is a relationship between two or more people who enjoy each others company and have trust in one another.** Ask the students to think about a time when someone was a friend to them. Spend a little time letting the students share their stories with the class.

Activity C–Friendship Circle

Select 10 students from the class to come to the front of the room and stand in a circle. Instruct each student to reach out with his/her left hand and take the hand of someone across the circle from them. Then grab the hand of someone else with their right hand. When all of the students have a hold of two hands, the fun begins. The goal is to sort out the circle without ever letting go of each others hands. They can climb over or go under peoples arms, but cannot release their hands. The bond between good friends can be as unbreakable as this circle.

Activity D–Read story about Dolphin

Dolphins are very playful mammals. They like to play with other animals like turtles, fish or birds. Dolphins are also known to be good friends with people. There are even stories about Dolphins saving people who were drowning or stranded at sea. Dolphins see with their ears by listening to their own echoes. With this type of radar, they are able to tell the size, shape, speed, distance and direction of other things in the water. Dolphins live in groups called pods, a type of large family. They will defend and take care of each other. When it is time for a baby to be born, other female Dolphins gather to protect them. Since Dolphins are mammals and need oxygen from air and not from water, as fish do, babies must be brought up to the surface to survive. After the birth, the baby must breath right away, so the mother pushes the baby to the surface with the help of other Dolphin friends. Dolphins look out for each other, enjoy one another, and can trust other Dolphins in their time of need.

Activity E–Silhouette Activity

Prepare ahead of time a large piece of butcher paper cut out in the shape of one of the student's silhouettes. Hang the cut-out up on the chalkboard. Tell the students that the silhouette is named "Bob". Have them come up one by one and write a mean put down about Bob somewhere on the silhouette **in pencil**. Then after they have completed writing their put down, have them tear off the portion of the silhouette where they wrote and take it back to their seat. When everyone has completed this task, there shouldn't be much of Bob left. Ask the students the following question. What did they do to Bob? Tell them that they literally tore him apart with their put downs. Now have them erase their negative comment and rewrite a positive one and bring their piece of Bob back to the front of the class. One by one, have the students tape him back together until the silhouette of Bob is whole again.

Ask the students to tell you how Bob looks now that he is taped back together. Does he look the same as he did when we first started? They should all see that although he is back in one piece, he is not the same as he was when we began. This represents how negative put downs can hurt a person deep inside. You can say you are sorry, but your harsh words will always leave a mark. Tell the students that before they put down another person or say something unkind, they should think to themselves, "How is what I am about to say going to affect this person"?

In summarizing the lesson, lead a discussion tying in friendship with bullying. Ask the students what they would do if they saw someone being a bully to a friend. To have a good friend, you must be a good friend. Think about what kind of friend you want to be, and if you act upon it, you will have no trouble making great friendships.

FOR ALL OF THE 6TH GRADE STUDENTS

Ask the class how they feel about going to Junior High School. Ask them if they are nervous or excited. Ask them the reasons they might be nervous and lead a class discussion about how they can turn their worries around. Discuss topics such as; not knowing where their classes are, not seeing familiar faces, bullies, etc. Help them solve these problems by; going to the school before hand, meeting new friends, staying away from bullies, etc. This discussion will be helpful for the students transition to a new environment.

(The journals are for the students to keep.)

Tell the students that you have enjoyed teaching them about self-esteem and hope they have really learned some valuable lessons. These lessons will help them with their future happiness and they have the tools now to have great self-esteem.

Pass out remaining Spotlight papers.